Pride

For over a decade, The New York Public Library and Oxford University Press have annually invited a prominent figure in the arts and letters to give a series of lectures on a topic of his or her choice. Subsequently these lectures become the basis of a book jointly published by the Library and the Press. For 2002 and 2003 the two institutions asked seven noted writers, scholars, and critics to offer their own "meditation on temptation" on one of the seven deadly sins. *Pride* by Michael Eric Dyson is the seventh and last book from this lecture series.

Previous books from The New York Public Library/Oxford University Press Lectures are:

The Old World's New World by C. Vann Woodward
Culture of Complaint: The Fraying of America by Robert Hughes
Witches and Jesuits: Shakespeare's Macbeth by Gary Wills
Visions of the Future: The Distant Past, Yesterday, Today, Tomorrow
by Robert Heilbroner
Doing Documentary Work by Robert Coles
The Sun, the Genome, and the Internet by Freeman J. Dyson
The Look of Architecture by Witold Rybczynski
Visions of Utopia by Edward Rothstein, Herbert Muschamp,
and Martin E. Marty.

Also by Michael Eric Dyson

Come Hell or High Water:
Hurricane Katrina and the Color of Disaster
(2006)

Is Bill Cosby Right?
Or Has the Black Middle Class Lost Its Mind?
(2005)

Mercy, Mercy Me:
The Art, Loves and Demons of Marvin Gaye
(2004)

The Michael Eric Dyson Reader
(2004)

Why I Love Black Women
(2003)

Open Mike:
Reflections on Philosophy, Race, Sex, Culture and Religion
(2003)

Holler If You Hear Me:
Searching for Tupac Shakur
(2001)

I May Not Get There With You:
The True Martin Luther King, Jr.
(2000)

Race Rules:
Navigating the Color Line
(1996)

Between God and Gangsta Rap:
Bearing Witness to Black Culture
(1996)

Making Malcolm:
The Myth and Meaning of Malcolm X
(1995)

Reflecting Black:
African-American Cultural Criticism
(1993)

Pride

The Seven Deadly Sins

Michael Eric Dyson

The New York Public Library

OXFORD
UNIVERSITY PRESS

2006

OXFORD
UNIVERSITY PRESS

Oxford University Press, Inc., publishes works that
further Oxford University's objective of excellence
in research, scholarship, and education.

Oxford New York
Auckland Cape Town Dar es Salaam Hong Kong Karachi
Kuala Lumpur Madrid Melbourne Mexico City Nairobi
New Delhi Shanghai Taipei Toronto

With offices in
Argentina Austria Brazil Chile Czech Republic France Greece
Guatemala Hungary Italy Japan Poland Portugal Singapore
South Korea Switzerland Thailand Turkey Ukraine Vietnam

Copyright © 2006 by Michael Eric Dyson

Published by Oxford University Press, Inc.
198 Madison Avenue, New York, NY 10016
www.oup.com

Oxford is a registered trademark of Oxford University Press

Library of Congress Cataloging-in-Publication Data
Dyson, Michael Eric.
Pride : the seven deadly sins / Michael Eric Dyson.
   p. cm. — (The seven deadly sins)
Includes bibliographical references and index.
ISBN-13: 978-0-19-516092-5
ISBN-10: 0-19-516092-4
1. Pride and vanity.
2. Deadly sins.
I. Title.
II. Seven deadly sins (Oxford University Press)
BV4627.P7D97 2006
241'.3—dc22   2005021049

Interior illustrations by Patrick Arrasmith / www.marlinaagency.com

9 8 7 6 5 4 3 2 1
Printed in the United States of America
on acid-free paper

Contents

Editor's Note

This volume is part of a lecture and book series on the Seven Deadly Sins cosponsored by the New York Public Library and Oxford University Press. Our purpose was to invite scholars and writers to chart the ways we have approached and understood evil, one deadly sin at a time. Through both historical and contemporary explorations, each writer finds the conceptual and practical challenges that a deadly sin poses to spirituality, ethics, and everyday life.

The notion of the Seven Deadly Sins did not originate in the Bible. Sources identify early lists of transgressions classified in the fourth century by Evagrius of Pontus and then by John of Cassius. In the sixth century, Gregory the Great formulated the traditional seven. The sins were ranked by increasing severity, and judged to be the greatest offenses to the soul and the root of all other sins. As certain sins were subsumed into others and similar terms were used interchangeably according to theological review, the list evolved to include the seven as we know them: Pride, Greed, Lust, Envy, Gluttony, Anger, and Sloth. To counter these violations, Christian theologians classified the Seven Heavenly Virtues— the cardinal: Prudence, Temperance, Justice, Fortitude, and the theological: Faith, Hope, and Charity. The sins inspired medieval and Renaissance writers, including Chaucer, Dante, and Spenser, who personified the seven in rich and memorable characters. Depictions grew to include associated colors, animals, and punishments in hell for the deadly offenses. Through history, the famous list has emerged in theological and philosophical tracts, psychology, politics, social criticism, popular culture, and art and literature. Whether the deadly seven to you represent the most common human foibles or more serious spiritual shortcomings, they stir the imagination and evoke the inevitable question—what is *your* deadly sin?

Our contemporary fascination with these age-old sins, our struggle against or celebration of them, reveals as much about our continued desire to define human nature as it does about our divine aspirations. I hope that this book and its companions invite the reader to indulge in a similar reflection on vice, virtue, the spiritual, and the human.

Elda Rotor

Preface

When I was invited by Oxford University Press and the New York Public Library to address one of the seven deadly sins, I knew immediately that I wanted to talk and write on pride. Perhaps it was a bit of vanity on my part: I had been thinking and, to a degree, writing about various forms of pride indirectly over the years and felt up to tackling the subject. Plus, I wanted to honor my teachers—especially Mrs. James, my fifth-grade teacher, who first gave me a sense of pride about black achievement; Mr. Burdette, my seventh-grade English teacher, who taught me to take pride in my oratory; and Mrs. Harvey, Mrs. Reed, Ms. Williams, Ms. Stewart, Mrs. Click, Mrs. Sutton, Madame Black, and a host of others—whose often unheralded efforts made a difference in their students' lives.

I also chose the most deadly of the seven sins because I wanted to deepen my engagement with pride, not only as a philosophical and religious idea but especially as a racial and national force. I have been shaped in a culture that has from the beginning struggled with its identity—with protecting itself against vicious assault while projecting its best features on a historical canvas marred by stereotype and willful ignorance of our virtues. I have feasted from birth on a black religious tradition that practices critical patriotism, or the love of country as an odyssey in dissent and truth-telling. To be sure, one runs the risk of being called unpatriotic, but then, claims of our unfitness to be either fully human or completely American are cruelly familiar. As for the advocates of white pride, unquestioning national pride, and their victims, Simone Weil's words on the use of might, which are just as true about pride, are instructive. "The strong are never absolutely strong, nor are the weak absolutely weak. Those who have Might on loan from fate count on it too much and are destroyed. Might is as pitiless to the man who possesses it (or thinks he does) as it is to its victims. The second it crushes, the first it intoxicates."

In my youth, black musicians and rhetorical artists provided the soundtrack to the struggle for self-respect and self-determination. Curtis Mayfield, who had already penned the love song "I'm So Proud," composed "We're a Winner," inspiring black folk to press on "Like your leaders tell you to" and "Keep On Pushing," singing "What's that I see, a great big stone wall, stands there ahead of me / But I've got my pride, and I'll move on aside, and keep on pushin'." And the magnificent voice and regal presence of Aretha Franklin shook our souls into pride and the demand for self-respect, even as, later, Stevie Wonder's symphonic suites of soul insisted that we proudly acknowledge the overlooked creators of history. Our orators, too, have been crucial to the cause, whether in the pulpit, the political forum, or the courtroom. Jesse Jackson conjures the vital spirit of resistance and self-affirmation when he declares, memorably, simply, but eloquently, and with great fire, "I am somebody," as he tirelessly continues the fight he began more than forty years ago to make the dream of freedom a reality. And the late Johnnie L. Cochran Jr.— through his heroic work in the legal system to defend the vulnerable and nameless as well as the high and notorious, and by his very style and humble, radiant presence—made elegant arguments on our behalf that resonated far beyond the halls of justice. Finally, the late John H. Johnson transformed the image of black people in America and around the globe through his publishing empire, especially *Ebony* and *Jet* magazines. Mr. Johnson also revolutionized the self-understanding of black folk by feeding us a steady diet of heroes, champions, spokespeople, entertainers, athletes, educators, reformers, revolutionaries, and martyrs. It is to these last five giants that I lovingly dedicate my book, for the pride they take in the great work they have offered, and for inspiring millions more to take pride in themselves.

This small book, and the series it appears in, wouldn't exist without Elda Rotor, of Oxford University Press, and Betsy Bradley of the New York Public Library, both of whom take great pride in the good work of their respective institutions. I am grateful to them both—and I am so proud of Elda, whom I have watched rise through the editorial ranks and receive well-deserved kudos for her talent, and whose suggestions brought conceptual clarity to this project as it unfolded. I am also grateful to Catherine Humphries and to Mary Sutherland for helpful editorial suggestions. I am thankful to Paul Farber, who provided helpful research assistance. I am thankful as well to my family, including my mother,

Addie Mae Dyson, and my brothers, Anthony, Everett (God bless you and keep you safe and strong), Gregory, and Brian, and my nieces and nephews. I am thankful as well for Michael Eric Dyson II, in whom I take great pride as he rises to the challenge of his vocation and manhood, and for Mwata, Maisha, Cory, and of course, for Marcia—I am so proud of how your intellectual and spiritual genius will now shine before the world.

Pride

Introduction
Enduring Pride

Of all the deadly sins, pride is most likely to stir debate about whether it is a sin at all. After all, without a sense of pride, one might not achieve or continue to strive for excellence in one's field of endeavor. Pride is certainly the catalyst for heroic deeds in sports; why else would Michael Jordan come back to basketball after winning three NBA championships to claim three more? Sure, his athletic pride had been wounded because he failed to master big-league baseball when he gave it a try after temporarily quitting the hardwood. But he proved he was a bigger man than his fans realized when he was willing to put aside his pride to chase a childhood dream to become one of the boys of summer. Even when it is considered a virtue, it is obvious, as in the Jordan example, that pride can have many functions, some of them contradictory. Pride drove Jordan back to basketball even as it failed to keep him from leaving the game in the first place. If pride is a sin, it is no ordinary sin, to be sure.

If one concedes that pride can be trouble, there is always the question if that is all there is to it. For instance, when it comes to defining the virtuous person, pride, often seen as a vice, might be a necessary feature of her identity. As philosopher Lawrence Becker argues, "If the virtuous person is in fact superior to vicious ones and if part of her virtue consists in having knowledge of such things, then it seems as though some dimension of pride is necessarily built into virtuous character."[1] In this case, at least, the stereotypical version of humility might not be the absolute virtue it is said to be, and pride might not be simply a vice. A more realistic view of ordinary moral behavior suggests that our definition of sin—or its opposite—must be vigorously complex. It is undeniable that the tough cases most stringently test our theories of virtue and vice. But even when dealing with knotty issues like race, religion, and nationalism, pride is rarely a simple matter, even when it is apparent that far more harm than good is in the offing.

In some cases, pride and the other deadly sins seem to be, if not conceptually obsolete, then certainly on the way out. According to a recent BBC poll, a majority of the British public "no longer believe that the Seven Deadly Sins have any relevance to their lives and think they should be brought up to date to reflect modern society."[2] The poll suggests that the original cardinal sins—anger, gluttony, sloth, envy, pride, lust, and greed—no longer hold sway as they once did and should be replaced by a "new list of contemporary taboos" that "capture the essence of modern morality."[3] Cruelty led the new list, followed by adultery, bigotry, dishonesty, hypocrisy, greed (the only original sin retained), and selfishness.

The Catholic Church of Scotland was unimpressed with the British public's modern sense of sin, which, according to a spokesman, was decidedly relativistic. "The new list is an interesting variation of the first, but introducing people to the concept of sin has well and truly disappeared. Scotland is driven by moral relativism and it has reached a point where right and wrong do not figure in most people's lives. The more important thing is to reintroduce the concept of sin and the fact that there are moral rights and wrongs."[4] Peter Donald, the convener of the panel of doctrine for the Church of Scotland, made a further distinction that accounted for the Church's resistance to the newfangled sins. "I find it interesting that the top three of the new sins are ones that affect others when we commit them," Donald said. "The original list dealt mainly with those which offend God, though that isn't to say this one wouldn't, but it is a symptom of humanistic morality."[5]

The claims by Scottish churchmen that the new sins are relativistic and humanistic are unsurprising, though still disappointing. I think that the classic list of sins still holds up after more than fourteen hundred years. But the attempt by the British public to update the sin list reflects the earnest desire to make the notion of sin more relevant to their lives, not to lose it in a haze of ethical contingency. I find it reassuring that folk are still wrestling with the notion of sin at all: not the hellfire-and-brimstone variety of many religious bodies but the concrete act of failing a moral obligation to others and God. Of course, on the face of things, it looks as if God has been banished, but just as with school prayer, God doesn't have to be officially on the premises in order to do good work. And my religious tradition quotes a scripture that says, "If a man say, I love God, and hateth his brother, he is a liar: for he that loveth not his brother whom he hath seen, how can he love God whom he hath not seen? And this commandment have we from him, That he who loveth God love his brother also."[6]

Thus, the treatment of human beings is a critical plank in the Christian platform of defining and overcoming sin. A morality that attempts to please God without attending to its effect on the human beings that God loves may ultimately do more harm than those moral visions that claim no truck with the Almighty, but which nevertheless achieve the work of the Kingdom. In this era of global relations, God may be theologically outsourcing the pursuit of justice, truth, and goodness to those without religious portfolio who are willing to do the work. If we keep the old list of sins but don't address racial bigotry, for instance, or personal hypocrisy, or corporate dishonesty, then the list is of little use to those who seek guidance and training in living and doing right.

In the United States, at least in pop culture, it seems the seven deadly sins, according to one newspaper, "are suddenly hotter than you-know-where."[7] The paper boasts that "MTV's 'Road Rules' challenge involves navigating an obstacle course based on the naughty behavior that can divert an otherwise good soul from the straight and narrow," and that "Broadway soprano Audra McDonald's concert series—knitting together songs about the various forms of banned behavior—debuted . . . at Carnegie Hall" while "on HBO we learned another soprano—Tony Soprano—suffers the deadly vice of pride."[8] The paper runs through all seven deadly sins, beginning, in good theological fashion, with vanity, a "form of pride, the sin 'from which all others arise,'" boasting that "vanity's just plain healthy, as far as we're concerned," while recommending a slew of spas that will assure that "[y]our mirror, mirror on the wall has never seen a more beautiful babe."[9]

If such a description trivializes pride and the seven deadly sins, others still see in their catalogue of moral travail "a yardstick for measuring the health of a culture."[10] Psychotherapist Philip Chard says of pride that given "our national plague of entitlement combined with our go-it-alone approach to the world, I'd say we're full of ourselves." He claims that we are "bedeviled with narcissists, egomaniacs and spoiled brats," and that "[o]minously, excessive pride, individual and collective, has preceded the demise of most of the world's great empires."[11] Pride has not exhausted its usefulness as either a playful reference for self-indulgence or a moral beacon to warn individuals and nations against the plague of untamed arrogance.

It is remarkable how rhetorically pliable pride is, how it is linguistically and conceptually adaptable to a vast array of emotional, moral, and intellectual circumstances. There are the sorts of pride one may experience: lost, wounded, hurt, restored, simple, foolish, lasting, injured, false, fatherly, mother's, and justifiable pride. There are prepositional prides that dot the landscape: pride in, of, for, and over. There are the conjunctional prides: pride and joy, and pride and sorrow. There are prides that show action in verbs: shining and beaming pride. There are prides that speak of loss and plenitude: lack of pride and full of pride. There are symptoms and manifestations of pride as well: the badge, mark, sign, and legacy of pride. And there are negative synonyms of pride—arrogance, vanity, and hubris—and positive cognates for pride, such as self-respect, self-esteem, and dignity.[12]

This profusion of forms suggests that pride still resonates in modern cultures. Through its striking prisms we can glimpse the multifaceted moral force that breaks and builds persons, institutions, cultures, and nations. The notion of pride is perhaps even more ethically useful to humans the world over now that we are living again through ethnic cleansings, holocausts, civil rights revolutions, famines, human rights struggles, wars, and all manner of terror. This book probes the philosophical, religious, personal, racial, and national roots of pride in the conviction that only when we tap its deeply entrenched sources can we combat the folly of pride with a vision of its edifying purpose.

And lastly (I may as well confess it, since my denial of it will be believed by nobody), perhaps I shall a good deal gratify my own vanity. Indeed, I scarce ever heard or saw the introductory words, "Without vanity I may say," &c., but some vain thing immediately followed. Most people dislike vanity in others, whatever share they may have of it themselves; but I give it fair quarter where I meet with it, being persuaded that it is often productive of good to the possessor, and to others that are within his sphere of action; and therefore, in many cases, it would not be altogether absurd if a man were to thank God for his vanity among the other comforts of life.

—Benjamin Franklin,
The Autobiography of Benjamin Franklin

The Virtuous Vice?
Philosophical and
Religious Roots of Pride

Is pride a good or bad thing? That depends on how we view the idea of pride, on what sources and history we cite, on what social and political contexts we view it in, on whether we're religious or secular, and on how we conceive of virtue and vice.

For several centuries, due in large part to Christian belief, pride has been seen as the deadliest of all sins. That wasn't always the case. In the earliest example of what we now term the seven deadly sins (called then the "chief" sins), pride and vainglory, which were still separated, came in fourth and fifth places in the "Testament of Reuben," a slice of the pseudepigraphy *Testament of the Twelve Prophets* (109–106 BC).[1]

Later, Evagrius of Pontus was one of the first Christian thinkers to refer to cardinal sins—there were eight of them in his reckoning—and vainglory and pride snagged the sixth and seventh spots on his list.[2] It wasn't until late in the sixth century that Pope Gregory I boosted pride to, well, its pride of place among the sins. Actually, it was *superbia*, the Latin equivalent of the Greek *hubris*, that Gregory isolated as the source of all sin, and *vana gloria*, or vainglory, led Gregory's list until the concepts were subsequently combined in "pride," which eventually earned the premium nod on most conventional lists.[3]

Gregory held that "pride is the root of all evil, of which it is said, as scripture bears witness: 'Pride is the beginning of all sin.' But even principal vices, as its first progeny, spring doubtless from this poisonous root. . . ."[4] Gregory argued that when "pride, the queen of sin, has fully possessed a heart, she surrenders it immediately to seven principal sins, as if to some of her captains, to lay it waste."[5] The core of pride, for Gregory, is an arrogance where man "favours himself in his thought; and . . . walks with himself along the broad spaces of his thought and silently utters his own praises."[6]

Perhaps few thinkers have exerted as much influence as has Augustine (334–430) on the Christian belief that pride is *the* fundamental sin.[7] Augustine maintained that an arrogant will led to original sin, and thus, pride is the first sin, temporally and theologically.[8] Pride caused man to turn away from God and to partially lose his being. "Yet man did not fall away to the extent of losing all his being; but when he had turned towards himself his being was less real than when he adhered to him who exists in a supreme degree."[9] For Augustine, pride encourages man to displace God, to act on the willful denial of human limitation, to covet unjust privileges, and to glory in self far too much.

> What could begin this evil will but pride, that is the beginning of all sin? And what is pride but a perverse desire of height, in forsaking Him to whom the soul ought solely to cleave, as the beginning thereof, to make the self seem the beginning. This is when it likes itself too well. . . . What is pride but undue exaltation? And this is undue exaltation, when the soul abandons Him to whom it ought to cleave as its end and becomes a kind of end in itself.[10]

For Augustine, the solution was for men to seek humility, since, "in a surprising way, there is something in humility to exalt the mind, and something in exaltation to abase it."[11] This Augustinian paradox is enlivened because he realizes that while humility causes the mind to be subject to what is superior—and nothing is superior to God, hence, humility causes the mind to be subject to God—exaltation abases the mind by spurring it to resist subjection to God. This is a character fault that leads to rebellion against God and places man in league with the devil's delusional desire to be like God.[12] Augustine concludes that "the original evil" occurs when "man regards himself in his own light, and turns away from that light which would make man himself a light if he would set his heart on it."[13]

Thomas Aquinas picked up on Augustine's themes, and on the beliefs of Gregory too, and gave them great prominence in his theology.[14] Aquinas understood pride as man's disordered desire to be exalted and as contempt for God seen clearly in the refusal to submit to God's divine rule.[15] This is why, for Aquinas, pride is both the foulest of sins and the mother of all the vices.[16] Moreover, Aquinas viewed pride as the excessive desire for one's excellence, yet another way to thwart the divine rule. As Eileen Sweeney argues, pride was the most lethal sin for Aquinas because it was first in moral intention and in its harmful effect.

> It is the worst sin, Aquinas argues, because it is of its very nature an aversion from God and his commandments, something that is indirectly or consequently true of all sins. Pride is the source of all other sins, Aquinas argues, in the sense that it is first in intention. First, every sin begins in turning from God and hence all sins begin in pride. Second, he argues, the motive for acquiring all the lesser goods one prefers to God is pride, that through them one "'may have some perfection and excellence." Covetousness is the first sin in the order of execution, Aquinas observes, since it desires what become the means for the commission of other sins. . . . Hence, the first sin must have been the coveting of some spiritual good, not ordinately but disordinately, "above one's mea-

sure as established by the Divine rule," and, Aquinas concludes, this pertains to pride.[17]

How, then, do people become appropriately subject to God? For Aquinas, it is through humility, a state where every person, "in respect of that which is his own, ought to subject himself to every neighbor, in respect of that which the latter has of God."[18] Humility has the virtue of withdrawing "the mind from the inordinate desire of great things against presumption."[19] The bottom line is that humility expresses the subordination of the human being to God.

One version or another of the Augustinian and Thomistic view of pride as the basic sin has held sway in Christian theology over the centuries, showing up as recently as the twentieth century in the writings of Reinhold Niebuhr. However, despite the thematic consistency across diverse Christian communities—pride is viewed as the basic sin in Roman Catholic parishes as well as in black Baptist churches—just what pride looks like and how it is best addressed is colored by the social and political contexts that shape faith and theology. In fact, there is considerable tension between Christian communities over the moral uses of competing explanations of pride.

For example, the abortion debate features on one side those Christians who claim that advocates of choice arrogantly seek to replace God by determining when life ends. On the other side are those Christians who claim that right-to-lifers proudly believe they know God's will, which is to protect the fetus at all costs. And when Martin Luther King Jr. claimed "cosmic companionship" in the struggle for social justice, he offered his followers a sort of compensatory pride that both addressed their vulnerable social status and perhaps implied that their opponents, including millions of white Christians, were on the wrong side of history—and God.

If the notion of pride as *the* mortal sin has worked its way through centuries of Christian belief, the philosophical view of pride has been equally interesting and influential. In fact, philosophical discussions of pride are older than much of Christian theology and have shaped the views of early theologians like Augustine and Aquinas. Of course, a big difference between theologians and philosophers is that the latter discussed pride in terms of vice rather than sin.

To be sure, religious thinkers like Aquinas theorized on pride in philosophical terms. Unlike most of his philosophical peers, however, he attempted to coordinate and reconcile conceptions of vice and sin.[20] Simply put, vice is a flaw in human nature as defined by reason, while sin is an offense to the law of God. In Aquinas's thinking, they were one in the same, since "to be against human nature, i.e., reason, is to be against the law of God."[21] By conceiving of pride as a vice, philosophers sought to judge moral practice by means of human reason and not divine revelation.

It was among the Greeks, although the concept is much older, that *hubris*—arrogant and unwarranted pride—was most strongly condemned.[22] Pride was widely denounced because it destroyed the cardinal virtues of courage, temperance, justice, and wisdom that buttressed the political order and made the good life possible.[23] Writers as varied as Homer, Herodotus, Aeschylus, Thucydides, and Plato viewed pride as the major vice and the primary source of poor moral judgment and political disaster.[24] Besides Greek figures, Roman, medieval, and early modern thinkers chimed in on the harmful effects of pride.

If the view of pride as a vice held sway over many Greek thinkers, it failed to draw Aristotle, at least not completely, into its fold. Aristotle famously caught sight of the prideful man, and for the most part, liked what he saw. In fact, he viewed pride as "the crown of the virtues."[25] Of course, his thinking on the matter can't be entirely separated from his aristocratic social views nor his sexist values, both of which result in an "appalling picture of the crown of the virtuous life."[26] Still, for verve and clarity, and for the ability to paint a picture of how, to paraphrase Sade (the singer, not the philosopher), pride is stronger than vice, few can rival Aristotle.

Aristotle claimed that the "proud man"—or in alternative translations, the "great-souled person," or the "magnanimous man"—is the one who "thinks himself worthy of great things, being worthy of them."[27] The proud man deserves what he claims, and if he is truly proud, never shirks from laying claim to what he deserves, since it is a vice to claim less than one deserves. But it is also wrong to claim *more* than one deserves, a vice that never befalls the truly proud. For Aristotle, "he who does so beyond his deserts is a fool, but no virtuous man is foolish or silly."[28] Men who deserve to be seen as morally great should recognize it and expect others to do the same. Truly proud men should be accorded their aristocratic due, but only because they have earned it through genuine merit, through moral superiority, and not through the fortune of good birth or wealth or power.

On the other hand, men of only moderate or even low moral achievement should accept their less celebrated lot, because "he who is worthy of little and thinks himself worthy of little is temperate, but not proud."[29] Should the lower moral-achieving man seek recognition beyond his desert, he should be viewed as vain or conceited.[30] As D. S. Hutchinson argues, the "problem with the vain man is not that he claims too much respect, but that he does not deserve it enough, and he tends to confuse the outward marks of dignity with dignity itself."[31] Alternatively, the man who thinks he is worthy of less than he really is, is "unduly humble" and "little-souled."[32] Aristotle despises such undue humility because the humble man thinks he deserves less than he does, and thus fails to appreciate his true worth. Aristotle prefers vanity to humility—and thinks the true opposite of pride is undue humility—because the latter is "both commoner and worse."[33]

But owning up to one's true moral achievement and expecting others to follow suit is by no means an act of vanity or conceit. The virtue of pride, or, as Aristotle terms it, "proper pride," is the mean found between extremes of empty vanity and undue humility.[34] Because desert is measured in relation to external goods, Aristotle deems it worrisome that men should seek to be honored too much, and by the wrong men, since honor is "surely the greatest of external goods."[35] To be worthy of honor is the prize of virtue, and, therefore, pride is the crown of virtues because "it makes them greater."[36] Of course, Aristotle presumes that the proud man claims and deserves the most because he possesses all the other virtues.[37]

The preoccupation by philosophers and other writers with the vice of pride—from Alexander Pope ("In pride, in reas'ning pride, our error lies") to Jonathan Swift ("but when I behold a lump of deformity, and diseases both in body and mind, smitten with pride, it immediately breaks all the measures of my patience"); from David Hume ("any expression of pride or haughtiness, [in others] is displeasing to us, merely because it shocks our own pride, and leads us by sympathy into a comparison, which causes the disagreeable passion of humility") to Spinoza ("The greatest pride or dejection indicates the greatest weakness of mind")—has been especially poignant when virtue has been seen as vital to ethical reflection.[38]

In the seventeenth and eighteenth centuries, for example, despite the complex variety of beliefs explored by representative thinkers, "in general, pride is condemned because it is unsocial; and because it is based on ignorance and falsehood. In particular, first, pride was made to bear the odium and responsibility of giving rise to cruelty and madness, and other dependent moral evils; and, second, as a violent passion itself, it was regarded, at least potentially, as the negation of reason and virtue."[39]

It seems that debate about pride has thrived when there was wide enough understanding in the culture that virtue, even if called by some other name, was worth the energy it would take to pursue high moral achievement. Of course, that's not a state of affairs we can take for granted, especially if we agree with philosopher Alasdair MacIntyre and Christian ethicist Stanley Hauerwas that a version of ethical philosophy that prizes rules and principles over the theory of virtue held sway in society for far too long. In fact, as late as 1973 it was not uncommon in philosophical circles for the concept of virtue to be described as "an old-fashioned but still useful term."[40] The early 1970s were not marked by huge leaps in moral philosophy that troubled over the sort of persons people become while making moral choices. The profession was yet in the throes of moral reasoning that gave most of its attention to the consequences of moral choice. Or else it was mired in generating rules and principles to decide between competing ethical options. In either case, moral philosophy had largely forsaken virtue ethics.

But in 1982, with the publication of MacIntyre's seminal *After Virtue*, the kind of moral philosophy that prized virtue and embraced Aristotle made a big comeback.[41] For MacIntyre, philosophy was not about identifying the moral properties of arguments. Neither was it stuck on clarifying the relevant linguistic snags and logical contradictions of such arguments. And it surely wasn't obsessed with justifying the selection of one moral option over the next. MacIntyre insisted that moral theory shed its enchantment with a liberal individualism spawned by the Enlightenment. He also gave thumbs down to the accompanying myth of the autonomous moral agent. Moral philosophy was about pursuing the virtues. Such an enterprise makes sense only in communities that share a common moral experience and vocabulary.

At the same time, Stanley Hauerwas insisted that virtue is central to Christian morality in powerful books like *Character and the Christian Life, Vision and Virtue, A Community of Character,* and *The Peaceable Kingdom.*[42] Hauerwas assailed the "decisionist ethics" that had choked contemporary Christian and secular moral philosophy. He argued instead that narratives hold together Christian ethics. After all, the stories that Christians tell shape human identity. These same stories make clear that moral meaning flows from the story of God's activity in human history.

Does any of what we have so far discussed—reflections on pride by Gregory, Augustine, Aquinas, and Aristotle, and MacIntyre's and Hauerwas's views on virtue—have any bearing on flesh-and-blood moral issues, or on life-and-death struggles today? Undoubtedly, at key moments in our nation's history, arguments and struggles over virtue have emerged: in the fight for racial justice in the civil rights struggle, for instance, or in the decision to use nuclear weapons in World War II. Though the fiercely pitched battles around national crises may not refer explicitly to virtue ethics—or to pride, or justice and courage in the way that philosophers and religious critics refer to these and other habits that make up virtue's moral bounty—the ideas it unleashes have impact far beyond the realm of professional philosophy. Still, it can't be denied that there is often a severe disconnection between debate of these ideas in religious and philosophical circles, and their application in the bloody world of culture and politics. Such a circumstance might lead to the conclusion that debates about pride, as vice or sin, have no relevance today. But that would be misleading.

For me personally, and I suspect for millions more like me whose religion shaped their morality (I am a Christian and ordained Baptist minister), the notion of pride as a deadly sin continues to resonate. I can remember many sermons and Sunday school lessons warning me and my peers against the presumptuousness that was pride's bitter fruit, a presumptuousness that might rage out of control in excessive self-regard and self-celebration. Hence, Proverbs 16:18 was a foundational scripture: "Pride goeth before destruction, and a haughty spirit before a fall."[43] And in various church settings—a visiting revivalist's fiery orations in the sanctuary, a conference for Sunday school students, the denomination's annual convention—the Augustinian and Thomistic view of pride was preached into us until we were able to recite its theological roots by heart: human pride is often a roadblock to divine order, and only those wise enough to surrender to God's guidance could truly benefit from the blessing of a life subject to God's word and way.

It was when those lessons got colloquial—when European theology was dipped into the healing waters of black vernacular and baptized in the truth of black life—that they were brought home with verbal excitement and moral force. Preachers and teachers never tired of raising with the Psalmist the question, "What is man, that thou art mindful of him? and the son of man, that thou visitest him?"[44] One preacher memorably interpreted this scripture along with a famous passage in Job ("Where were you when I laid the foundation of the earth?" God asks Job) to remind us that God is in control and the author of the universe. "You've got to remember, brothers and sisters," the minister thundered at our youthful ears, "when it comes to ultimate truth and the counsels of wisdom before the Almighty, your pride has to take a back seat and you've got to realize, *you ain't all that!*"[45]

We were taught that individuals are not the only ones to become ensnared in pride; nations, too, spiral down the stairway of arrogant behavior into sinful excess. There was a strong emphasis in my church, and in many other black churches, on the notion that nations were scarcely beyond God's judgment. Further, we often heard from the most prophetic ministers in our churches that America must be painfully conscientious in flexing its muscle in the world. Since the nation had often acted to crush its very own citizens of color, it must work even more zealously to rid itself of the belief in its "Manifest Destiny" as the apple of God's eye.

This view is nicely captured in the Chris Rock film *Head of State*, when a fictional film character running against Rock for the presidency habitually closed his speeches with the plea, "God bless America, *and no place else!*" Indeed, bitter disputes over the moral status of the nation and of the function of religion in sanctifying or challenging the state have divided believers of all faiths who hold competing views of national pride. Just how does one love one's country, and should such love exceed one's love of God? Although the answer to the latter query appears to be a simple no, the difficulty arises when love of God and country are fatally blurred, and theology becomes little more than a handmaiden of empire.

Then, too, secular citizens must often feel that religious folk have become trapped by the very pride that Gregory, Augustine, and Aquinas warned us against. It is the ugly face of pride that glowers in self-righteous disdain at all who fall beyond its pale. The result of such self-satisfaction is gruesome. It is glimpsed in the abrasive style many religious communities adopt to display the truths of the faith. It burns in the desire to build a kingdom of self-enclosed spiritual power and material wealth. It is also stamped in the loss of a healthy skepticism about one's own religion and the poignant self-questioning that authentic faith breeds.

Such self-questioning, by the way, is characteristic of the best of all faith traditions; is just as true of Christianity as it is of Judaism, Islam, and Buddhism. Too often, however, we elevate our faith to such heights that one can honestly ask if what is being worshipped is really one's church, ashram, temple, synagogue, or mosque, rather than the God to which they all point. Pride in one's religion, in how one understands and serves God, is just as great a distortion of the faith as those habits that obviously divide one from God.

This is why, perhaps, the concept of vice is a secular check on the pride of religious folk in determining what and who is sinful. (And it might just be God's way of sneaking in some moral philosophy on the proud person and sinner alike.) It's not that sin should be ditched as a viable category of spiritual and moral critique; it's just that we've got to be held accountable, not only to God but to other human beings. If they are not one and the same for religious folk, they are close enough to warrant a rethinking of the harsh separation of theology and anthropology. To this end, the late church historian James Washington's words are entirely apropos: some of us go to church "to love God *instead* of our neighbor."[46]

But if some of us run to religion to escape our neighbors, many of us hide in our faith to avoid thinking about it or the problems we face. It is true that one of the vicious consequences of pride is that human reason threatens to replace divine revelation in the religious worldview. Such a claim, however, is subject to reason. Articulate defenders of faith have rightly attempted to sidestep vicious circularity by contending that conceptions of truth are a species of the good; what we know as true is in part a product of what we think is good to know. The value of knowledge is made clear when we define the moral properties of the world we live in and seek to understand. That doesn't completely solve the problem; for instance, some seekers limit the quest for truth to what their religion says is good while ignoring the common good. But at least it offers a reasonable way to hold to faith while honoring the mind God gave us.

One version of pride argues that intellectual activity is an affront to a God who demands that believers surrender reason at the doorway of faith. But that is often little more than a cover for lazy anti-intellectualism masquerading as resistance to excessive pride. Arthur Lovejoy says that in the eighteenth century "it became customary to berate and satirize all forms of intellectual ambition, and to ascribe to it a great part in the corruption of the natural innocence of mankind . . . [t]he condemnation of 'pride,' then, is frequently . . . one of the ways of expressing a primitivistic anti-intellectualism."[47]

In our own day, too, literalists, fundamentalists, reactionaries, and rigid conservatives of all faiths lash out at the intellect as the source of sinful pride. They deny reason a virtuous role in serving truth, courage, justice, and love. There is, however, a healthy skepticism in religious circles about enshrining reason as an idol or fetish. As I was constantly reminded in church—especially by my brilliant pastor and mentor, Dr. Frederick Sampson—we must "love the Lord thy God with all thy heart, and with all thy soul, and with all thy mind, and with all thy strength," and therefore be better able to "love thy neighbor as thyself."[48] Thinking too highly of oneself is a sin; thinking well of God and others, and therefore of oneself, is a sacrament.

Aristotle's view of "proper pride," of avoiding both undue humility and empty vanity, helps to clarify how healthy self-regard is a vital pillar to love of God and neighbor. If thinking too highly of oneself is a sin, then the Aristotelian vice of thinking too lowly of oneself qualifies as well. At a minimum, it signifies a rejection of God's creation, even if the creature is the source of doubt about her worth. Thus, to take pride in one's person, one's achievements, one's moral worth—and not, as Aristotle suggested, one's fortunate birth or power or wealth—is to affirm and embrace the character of God reflected in one's own soul.

More painfully, self-rejection increases the chances of other-rejection. If I fail to love myself, the self that God made and loved, then I will likely fail to recognize the God and worth in others. (At many of the black churches where I preach, there is a lovely tune sung when visitors are announced, with the refrain, "The Jesus in me, loves the Jesus in you," accompanied by hand gestures to self and others. It may seem hokey, but it is a vital affirmation of the principle of mutuality and of finding worth in self and others because of the unifying presence of divine recognition in each.)

The stakes of self-regard are greatly increased when a healthy pride has been systematically denied an entire group of people, because of race, gender, sexual identity, age, and the like. That's why the loving, affirming black communities in which I was nurtured, and which told me stories, listened to my own, and encouraged me to tell them, are critical to my own self-worth and self-love. If MacIntyre and Hauerwas are right about the benefits of recovering virtue and about linking our reflections on the good life to the pursuit of virtue in communities that bring them alive, then the sorts of stories we tell ourselves in worship, and at school, home, and work, are vital to our psyches, our souls, and to our society.

The love of self I learned in the local Baptist church has an edifying effect on the public good. I am not only a better person but a better citizen as well, and a better participant in the various kinship groups to which I belong and that help define my identity and role in the culture. These stories of achievement told to me by my black teachers also made me appreciate hallowed traditions of survival and art in black culture.

Unfortunately, these traditions remain obscured by a fatal lack of curiosity about certain dimensions of black life or a deadening indifference to its vital complexity. My own writing, as I'll discuss in the next chapter, is a way of recounting the books that shaped me, the stories that fed me, and the ideas that filled me with hope; and it is a way of taking pride in joining a long list of venerable truth tellers. But those same stories trace an ethical edge that sometimes cuts against the grain and wounds the false pride of romantic accomplishments and slices through to the core of authentic achievement.

I suppose I still believe that pride can be a sin, and a deadly one, especially when it's wielded by unprincipled forces and immoral people. Pride is also a vice when it traffics in accomplishments that have little to do with genuine moral achievement but instead rest on the exercise of power or wealth. Pride is surely a vice, and a sin, when it is absent on faces twisted into self-loathing caricatures of abasement. Humility is virtuous, but humiliation, whether invited or imposed, is vicious.

Proper pride is a boon, a stroke of moral genius against those who would withhold its virtue in the false belief that they might increase their own. But every withheld honor does dishonor to those who hold back what others deserve, even if the transaction takes place within one's soul. Self-regard is a key to both our psychic strength and our moral health. For me, writing, and the reading upon which it rests, is a way to tell critical stories that strengthen self-regard—yes, I'm not too proud to admit, my own, and hopefully, that of others—while puncturing the vanity of power.

In the segregated schools of my growing up, to work hard at ones studies was a source of pride for the race and, though we did not understand it that way, for our class as well.

—bell hooks, *Where We Stand: Class Matters*

I have often asked myself: would I still write today if they told me that tomorrow a cosmic catastrophe would destroy the universe, so that no one could read tomorrow what I wrote today? My first instinct is to reply no. Why write if no one will read me? My second instinct is to say yes, but only because I cherish the desperate hope that, amid the galactic catastrophe, some star might survive, and in the future someone might decipher my signs. In that case writing, even on the eve of the Apocalypse, would still make sense. One writes only for a reader. Whoever says he writes only for himself is not necessarily lying. It is just that he is frighteningly atheistic. Even from a rigorously secular point of view. Unhappy and desperate is the writer who cannot address a future reader.

—Umberto Eco, "How I Write"

CHAPTER TWO

I Witness: Personal Pride

The pride I take in reading and writing books is, in part, a representative pride: it draws from and reflects the community of black folk who taught me to read and write. They also made me love learning, and they took great pride in my achievements along the way. My pride in what I do is also a way to repay the kindness of mentors who took me under wing. Thus, my pride is a spur to excellence; it inspires me to the virtue of writing and thinking well. My teachers took great pride in the fact that my reading and writing, my course of learning, would delve into black life while also probing the outlines of the wider world. I discovered in the process that the books I read or, rather, that read me, helped form in me a clearer picture of my place in the universe, and hence, boosted my esteem beyond even the measure of pride my mentors could give me. Where they left off, the books took up. Those noble souls who took pride in me deposited in me the hope that I might turn literacy into a weapon against the brutalizing forces of ignorance—of our community, our culture, and our race.

Of course, I didn't set out to be the sort of writer who observes society to change it, which is what social critics do. I suppose, in retrospect, I had two goals: to write like the writers I most admired, those writers my teachers pointed me to, and to write as well as I could about things that mattered most to me. When it comes to writing, even for social critics like me, reading is fundamental. I knew fairly early that I had no talent for writing fiction. Reading it, though, made me feel the hot breath of imagination. I never had to leave the house to leave home; I looked no farther than the page to see the world. I chased whales with Melville. I hugged gulags with Solzhenitsyn. I sank into the tongue of black preaching with Baldwin. Later, I sprouted wings and took to the sky with Morrison. And I skulked in bleak undergrounds with Dostoyevsky and Ellison.

When I first read *Invisible Man,* the only novel Ralph Ellison published during his lifetime, the first line cut through my tender teen mind like a sword.[1] He wrote: "I am an invisible man." It sliced me open and helped give shape to the vague, haunting outlines of race that I only barely grasped. I knew immediately that I had been found out by a book that had been written twenty years before it discovered me. I understood intuitively that the invisibility to which Ellison referred had to do with me, a poor black boy in Detroit's desperate ghetto.

If Ellison's first sentence was foundational, his fourth sentence was nearly jurisprudential, establishing the summary law of black life in a white world: "I am invisible, understand, simply because people refuse to see me." As I matured, I knew what it meant to live in the shadows, unperceived, unnoticed, an implausible figment of the American imagination. Still, I was fortunate enough early in my life to find protection in those black wombs of psychic resistance that Ellison limns in his eloquent narrative. Their pride in me was my protection; their insistent demand that I cope with my color by finding pride in my ability to fight back on page was one of their truest gifts to me.

The words of my black teachers and preachers sank me deeply into the soil of black spiritual edification, as do the words in Ellison's novel. And the jazz sounds—and the blues, too—that pass thickly through his text bathed me in their aura of black invincibility, defeating invisibility with the sublime confidence that black art forms possess. I especially took pride in Ellison's supremely accomplished wordplay and delighted in the sheer intellectual demand of his writing. He spoke elegantly of "the beautiful absurdity of American identity." Ellison unapologetically improvised his way through the history of ideas, nodding to Dostoyevsky with his main character's underground existence even as he later embraced T. S. Eliot in the title of his first and foremost collection of essays, *Shadow and Act*.[2]

But his originality consisted of the absolute insistence that the concept of America could never be wholly defined without extolling its central black presence. Even before I completely understood what he was up to, Ellison's gesture gave me a sense of pride that has never left me. To a black teen, the thought that the world wouldn't quite be the same without my people—which also, in some small way, meant me too—was a source of pride and immeasurably stabilizing. Ellison hammered away at this theme throughout *Invisible Man,* even showing the visible effects on white society of its suppressed dark side rising up to choke it nearly to death, as when the nameless main character nearly murders a white man who insults him. But Ellison's larger purpose, which he pursued through rigorous and beautiful essays, argued that white culture would be morally and spiritually isolated, even intellectually insufficient, without black life and thought.

If Ellison's opening sentences were magic to my mind and his language music to my ears, his closing words mark the ironic disappearance of invisibility as a symbolic barrier for younger blacks. Ellison ends his book with the memorable and infinitely interpretable sentence: "Who knows but that, on the lower frequencies, I speak for you?" Here, Ellison may be referencing an "everyman," but his words could easily be those of today's black youth culture that has, at points, been seen as incapable of speaking for bourgeois blacks. Hip-hop discourse might just be able to speak for black folk who don't ordinarily find themselves reflected in that world of banging rhythms and relentless speech. True enough, few blacks beyond the generational and geographical haunts of hip-hop take pride in its essential achievements—including lifting pavement poetry to an art form and telling compelling stories of marginalized but proud youth.

I think Ellison's phrase also has a message for black youth, whose problem is not invisibility but hypervisibility. Black youth are overseen through the surveillance of a dominant culture that at once desires and loathes them. Their styles flood the marketplace, from hip-hop music and speech to clothing and hair fashions. But their bodies increasingly fill detention halls and prison cells. If they have escaped invisibility as a condition of their oppression, black youth now suffer overexposure and stigma. There is little pride in such damning circumstances, and yet hip-hop has provided a powerful means of self-affirmation. And the source of genuine pride to many hip-hop aficionados—that its culture features gifted artists who are linked by theme and tone to earlier poets of black pride and revolution—is lost on many beyond the culture. In fact, at the core of the hypervisible black youth culture that now prevails are sides and views that get scarce airplay or screen time. After all, mainstream media is addicted to the thug and the materialist among hip-hoppers, while the griot and the spiritually attuned remain obscured.

Invisible Man still looms as a signifying text that is driven by the cycles and concurrences of seeing and unseeing to which blacks are subject. For even within the coarse and dismembering invisibility that Ellison outlined were ways of seeing each other that blacks have always relied on to support ourselves in hostile times. Hence, signifying, or insider language among initiated blacks, is a key to black survival, elements of which are liberally spread through Ellison's folklore-rich book. Whether black folk are in or out of style, *Invisible Man* always will be valuable in interpreting the trends that silhouette black life. And whether blacks suffer undervaluation or overexposure, *Invisible Man*'s thematic meditations will prove useful as a measure of artistic rebellion against the indifference to black life. Ellison's book is timeless because it refused to avoid the central problem of its own time. And since that problem—variously viewed as race, the politics of identity, and the relation of blackness to whiteness—has not gone away, neither, it seems, will Ellison's still charging classic.

Of course, there were other novels that gave me a sense of my moral and social possibilities, and which, as a result, deepened in me an Aristotelian sense of "proper pride." In 1977, when I was an eighteen-year-old, laid-off-from-work, welfare-receiving teen-father-to-be, an extraordinary gift of words arrived in my apartment: the book-club selection of Toni Morrison's *Song of Solomon*.[3] The book's brutal grace entranced me; its lyrical language effortlessly evoked a world teeming with magic and misery. Morrison helped me clarify the moral meaning of a black manhood under assault but never, at least not ultimately, out of control. It also made me proud to be a black man who desired to take flight. If a black man could fly, or want to, or even try and fail, then he was a black man who could wrest from his troubles, both imposed and self-created, a measure of humanity no one could take. That was a basis of pride no one could steal. I remembered that as I tucked *Song of Solomon* beneath my arm as I was evicted on Christmas Day. The signifying and sensuality of Morrison's sentences, and the intellectual demand that the reader be *present* and accounted for, have found their way into my own literary efforts over the years, whether a poem, a sermon, an essay, a book. Long before R. Kelly, she made black men proud to sing, "I believe I can fly."

Poetry made me yearn to warble the idioms that sprang from my heart, but I lacked the skill to clothe them in a language that made others want to sing along. I admired Tennyson greatly, perhaps Auden even more, and Wordsworth, the Brownings, Keats, Byron, Rilke, Roethke, and Brooks too. I won my first blue ribbon in the fifth grade for reciting from memory Paul Laurence Dunbar's vernacular verse. That was perhaps my proudest moment as a youth, especially because my fifth-grade teacher, Mrs. James, delighted so warmly in my victory.

But it was nonfiction writers that made me even hungrier to do what they did. (I must confess that it strikes me as a little odd to take up a kind of writing, "nonfiction," that defines itself in the negative, and that advertises its existence by referring to something it *isn't*. That's like thinking of life as "nondeath"). And it is the example of nonfiction writers whose art and craft have inspired in me a sense of excellence that, although rarely attained in my work, fills me with pride when I hit the mark. Since nonfiction takes up all the space outside of fiction's borders, there are a great number of genres and voices a writer might try on. I first quickened to the rhythms and idiosyncrasies of the critical voice when I trudged headlong and ill-equipped into a book about the transcenden-talists. I read this volume and others like it outside of my junior high school curriculum. Most of my new discoveries were retrieved from my weekly rummages in used book stores. I supplemented my habit in a daily tryst with the library turnstile inside my ghetto school. There I cornered Sartre and Santayana. Well, at least I grabbed them by the spines as I swam in their weird and challenging and thrilling words. I strove furiously to subdue their insights beneath my rapidly forming worldview. When I purchased William Barrett's *Irrational Man* and Walter Kaufman's sleekly edited *The Portable Nietzsche*, I slid into existentialism and the philosophical aphorism like a pair of comfortable jeans.

After that, the essay came calling. Emerson and Thoreau got me first. Then it was Montaigne, Renan, Burke, and even Abraham Lincoln, and whoever else tumbled from the pages of the *Harvard Classics* I had been given as a gift by my next door neighbor Mrs. Bennett after her husband died. She was so proud of my efforts to become widely literate that she sparked a deeper desire in me to become well-read. I also read Camus and caught a glimpse of Greek mythology sporting the apparel of Algerian absurdity. I drank in Bertrand Russell's fiercely eloquent words but not before noting his warning that the purpose of education is to resist the seductions of eloquence.

I discovered the voice of James Baldwin in 1970, and my life hasn't been the same since. I slept with Baldwin's essays like Coltrane slept with his horn, fingering in my own imagination the notes the writer played and charting the progression of chords in his symphonic meditation on the American soul.[4] I learned about Baldwin in Mrs. James's fifth-grade classroom, but when I crashed into his searing prose on the page, it was a train-wreck of revelation: about his life, and therefore mine, as a black male, about our common ghetto roots, and about the desire to sing of suffering and struggle with pitiless precision. I had inhaled his first and finest novel, *Go Tell It on the Mountain*, at age eleven, but later, at fourteen, *Notes of a Native Son* grabbed me by the brain and sent me reeling into passionate addiction.[5] I have read that book and all of Baldwin's essays, some of the finest in the English language, too many times, at too many different places in my life—joy and grief, adolescence and adulthood, amateur scribe and professor— to remember when I *haven't* read him for sanity and salvation. He made me proud to be a poor black boy whose hunger for reading and writing was insatiable and resolutely catholic.

I also got hooked on biographies, auto and otherwise. I sat in Benjamin Franklin's den as he dispensed wisdom and outlined the virtuous life. I learned even earlier about Martin Luther King Jr.'s heroism in Lerone Bennett's elegant prose. In 1968, when I was nine, Martin Luther King Jr. was assassinated, and I was eager, even desperate, to learn as much as I could about his life and what he meant to black folk—of all our majestic heroes, they appeared to be most proud of him—and the nation. I scurried to my Detroit elementary school library and found Bennett's *What Manner of Man: A Biography of Martin*

Luther King, Jr., a book that, when I opened it, opened my eyes to a world of racial conflict and moral courage that I barely knew.[6] Bennett's beautifully written biography of his former college classmate gave me a vivid impression of King and of the intellectual and social forces that drove him. I read that book time and time again; first, because it repeatedly sent me to the dictionary to learn new words, and second, because I was eager to learn more about a man who, besides my late pastor Dr. Sampson, had influenced me the most. When I wrote my own book on Dr. King, Bennett's model of careful scholarship and eloquent expression loomed large. I took no small pride (I hope it was "proper pride") when reviewers and readers found merit in my approach to King's protean spiritual and political journey.

Indeed, it was King's life that made me want to parse and embrace social redemption through the written word. King's pilgrimage was a moral lens on the social strife I barely understood. His inspiration found adolescent lungs in my first piece of writing, a speech I penned when I was eleven and delivered when I was twelve. Even before the literary lights of the ages flooded my youthful world, I burned with the desire to see brotherhood and love prevail. Before I wanted to write the world, I sought to right it. It's not that my love for King and the idea of social change made me any less exuberant about the writers I admired. Social criticism allowed me to split the difference between becoming a man of letters and a man of action—if not my own, then the inspiration for others. I resolved to transport the literate lessons of great writers to my bailiwick. One of them was not to take myself so seriously, even as I took my work with utter seriousness. That lesson reminds me to sidestep the humorless righteousness—the improper pride—that tempts the social critic's path.

I've got no illusion that writing social criticism is the equivalent of walking a picket line or delivering a fiery speech at a protest rally. I've done all three, and each has its place in the order of things. But there is supreme worth in engaging the issues of the day with the help of the intellectual and literary traditions we hold dear, or even the ones we ignore or despise. True, the payoff may not be as immediate as a vote in Congress. And the impact surely won't be as visible as the uplifting action of full-fledged social reformers like King or Gandhi (although both took up writing as social reform by other means), or even part-timers like Thoreau. That's why the social critic temporarily left Walden Pond and landed in his local jail: to flesh out his view that civil disobedience could help politics find a conscience. Most social critics will not be so lucky, or so brave, to follow the unsteady line that leads from the page to the public arena. But there is great virtue in writing well about the possibilities and obstacles in a democratic culture like ours. And when we do our jobs right, many others take great pride in our achievement, one that can range far beyond written words to well-trod paths of social action in the real world.

As a social critic, I have written a great deal about race and identity. (Besides occasionally donning a journalist's hat, I also write as a cultural critic, whose job is to examine aesthetic and moral effort with enlivened suspicion, and as a public intellectual, with the goal of casting a scholar's eye and a prophet's tongue on the rituals of citizenship and governance, although none of these modes of writing is clearly separated, and often, at least in my experience, they bleed profusely into one another). These subjects are central to the life of the nation. They also happen to be central to my life. My writing, therefore, has been pressured, though hopefully not trapped or disfigured, by social forces. That doesn't mean I can't stand at a distance from the events I observe. It means I don't stand at a *dangerous* distance, one clouded by the myth of neutrality or the belief that the critic can remain unscathed by the blisters of human striving. The hope for exemption from the swirl of life betrays a desire to stand outside of common limits like some moral Archimedes. At its best, social criticism is an inside job. The social critic must grasp our frailties even as he urges us to rise above their pull. She must know, like novelists know, that human life is born in story. She must hear with poets the metrics of sorrow and desire. And she must sense with playwrights the futility and ambition that spark a moral tug of war between head and heart.

Sometimes, the critic's job is thankless, or controversial, or more likely, both. This is where the shroud of false pride is torn off, and the duty to grind away mythologies, even of one's own tribe, rises up high. When I wrote my book on Martin Luther King Jr., a brigade of the leader's defenders and defamers emerged to miss my point. I didn't angle to put King down, as his largely right-wing and racist attackers had hoped. Neither did I seek to elevate him further into the mists of miscomprehending sainthood, as his mostly black true believers wished. I aimed to rescue King from the clutches of followers who worshipped him into irrelevance and opportunists who replaced his claws with mittens. King was a much more radical thinker than either friend or foe could tolerate. To say that well was the critical intention of my book. But I wasn't naïve; I had kept score, and I knew that those who had it in for King might try to use my book to support their devious assaults.

Still, as a social critic, I had to tell the truth about King—about his political genius and his moral guilt, about his fine and noble humanity as well as his failures and flaws. I trusted my fate as a critic to readers who would get my point after deep reflection over the long haul. I trusted them to treasure complexity above empty veneration, and in the end, to measure with me the outlines of King's true greatness. I suppose I drew this faith from the writers I had learned so much from, writers who knew that the truth well told, even if out of season, will ultimately find its way to those who are willing to pay the price to know it. But I didn't draw comfort only from the nonfiction writers whose mantle I have claimed. To paraphrase Tennyson, I am a part of all that I have read. Like Auden, whose poem "Musee Des Beaux Arts" was prompted by Brueghel's painting—which, in the poet's penetrating vision, reflects the fate of those who suffer and are lost at the edge of our awareness and compassion— our inspiration flows in from wherever we have found it or, more to the point, from wherever life has found us brave enough to confess our vulnerability. Reading great writing has inspired me as a social critic to write as best I can about what we human beings have been and should be. I hope that my writing can inspire others to do the same, and to act with conscience on their beliefs, especially in the effort to offset vicious forms of racial pride that mar the social compact. Should even a sliver of that hope prosper, I will take a small measure of pride in its achievement.

Since the beginning of the nation, white Americans have suffered from a deep uncertainty as to who they really are. One of the ways that has been used to simplify the answer has been to seize upon the presence of black Americans and use them as a marker, a symbol of limits, a metaphor for the "outsider." Many whites could look at the social position of blacks and feel that color formed an easy and reliable gauge for determining to what extent one was or was not American. Perhaps this is why one of the first epithets that many European immigrants learned when they got off the boat was the term "nigger"; it made them feel instantly American.

—Ralph Ellison,
"What America Would Be Like Without Blacks"

[T]here is, in fact, no white community. . . . No one was white before he/she came to America. It took generations, and a vast amount of coercion, before this became a white country. . . . Because they think they are white, they do not dare confront the ravage and the lie of their history. Because they think they are white, they cannot allow themselves to be tormented by the suspicion that all men are brothers. Because they think they are white, they are looking for, or bombing into existence, stable populations, cheerful natives and cheap labor. Because they think they are white, they believe, as even no child believes, in the dream of safety. Because they think they are white, however vociferous they may be and however multitudinous, they are as speechless as Lot's wife looking backward, changed into a pillar of salt.

—James Baldwin,
"On Being 'White' . . . And Other Lies"

CHAPTER THREE

Hubris and Hue:
White Pride

Long after the first wave of culture wars crashed American shores in the late 1980s, bitter debates about identity politics continue to ripple through the nation. Unfortunately, cultural myopia and historical distortion often follow in their wake. We are thus at a loss to explain the paradox of how identity politics have become at once popular and problematic. What the left and right conveniently forget is that identity politics were a problem long before blacks and other minorities gained limited power and visibility. If Aristotle's "proper pride" is a virtue to blacks whose self-respect has been battered, then white pride is often the vice that makes black pride necessary. This is as true for black folk in Boston as in Botswana, and just as relevant for whites in Bonn as in Bahia.

Pride in one's ethnic group has had a mixed history. For instance, Irish pride and Italian pride, although once scorned, are now widely embraced. Irish pride can make everyone who so wishes Irish for a day. Black pride has found a more difficult path to acceptance and has been quarantined in the racial ghetto. Black pride seems to possess a stingy singularity. Blackness continues to arouse deeply ambivalent feelings in the nation, and black identity, no matter how exotic or brilliant, can never entirely shed its stigma. Comedian Chris Rock once summed it up with a blistering aside when he said during a routine, "There ain't a white man in this room who'd change places with me . . . and I'm rich."[1]

If black pride, at least in the American scene, is unavoidably specific, the recent incarnation of white pride, when it can be defined as such, is subtle and pervasive, a largely amorphous force. To be sure, white pride, which exists only to thwart nonwhites, was openly embraced in a segregated past that decried the alleged perversities of black or native identities. Today it flares when the National Association for the Advancement of White People exaggerates the gains of minorities to boost the supposedly flagging esteem of white folk. Such groups, however, are no longer widely popular among whites. Still, it is difficult for many whites to acknowledge the transition from ethnic pride, a virtue, to white pride, a vice, although it has been persuasively documented in books like *How the Irish Became White* and *How Jews Became White Folks*.[2] The difficulty is compounded because most discussions of race in America center on what it means to be *nonwhite*. Very few whites are ever asked to think about what it means to be white or how whiteness defines so much of what we take for granted in the world.

White pride works best when it is not even up for discussion—when it can be denied as the purpose of talk or action and can be seen, instead, as the very framework of normal conversation and behavior. White pride here refers to how white life has been viewed as universal, while black life has been trapped, it is believed, by a negative particularity. White ways of speaking, thinking, and acting are the unerring standard of human achievement. The fact that these standards spring from particular ethnic communities has been successfully masked. As a result, whites have been able to criticize blacks, not for failing to be white but for their failure to be fully human.[3] In principle, of course, the two could hardly be distinguished, since whiteness, by fiat or force, consciously or unconsciously, is taken to be the norm—the dominant template of identity. Until the last fifteen years, whiteness has been spared the aggressive criticism that minority identities routinely receive.[4] Many critics of identity politics seem oblivious to this fact, or worse, willfully ignorant.

White pride has often been smuggled into national discourse under other labels: citizen, American, individual. Many whites, failing to see themselves as members of a race, define themselves as citizens, all the while denying that privilege to others. Whites are individuals and Americans; blacks, Latinos, Native Americans, and other minorities are viewed

as members of racial and ethnic subgroups. Whiteness has a doubly negative effect: it denies its racial roots while denying racial minorities their
American identities. The claims of white pride—to citizenship and to
the best jobs, schools, homes, and lives—are rarely framed in terms of
race. Instead, such claims are viewed as matters of individual merit, morality, politics, and economics. There is no need or desire to explicitly
refer to race in deciding who gets the lion's share of these resources. White
pride, therefore, is able to retain its force, its stalwart invisibility. Its advocates readily adopt the vocabulary of justice and national identity as
a means to reinforce their unspoken privilege. They are able to enjoy
such privilege while ostensibly being committed to the principle of
color-blindness that guided the civil rights movement.

Thus, such whites get two birds with one stone: They manage to
cast white pride as a matter of disinterested social policy while decrying
black claims to social goods as instances of race-conscious practices that
blacks sought to overthrow. If nothing else, such a move proves that
whiteness is slippery, adaptable, and malleable. And white pride in this
case is barely distinguishable from the simple pride of being a good American. In such a light, it makes perfect sense—indeed it seems inevitable—
that all identities that fall outside of the white mainstream are suspect.
This elaborately contrived ignorance of race that nevertheless shrewdly
exploits its existence invites scorn on minorities for tearing the social
fabric and "disuniting America."[5] Such charges are expected on the right;
they are becoming distressingly familiar on the left as well.

Before it became stylish to trumpet the artifice of race—that it is neither biologically based nor genetically transmitted, but created in society—most folk believed that whiteness was a relatively fixed identity. For blacks, the varied streams of whiteness flowed into one purpose: to contain, control, and at times, destroy black identity and pride. Whiteness became far more visible when assaulted black identities rebounded to challenge white authority. Ironically, the fate of whiteness was tied to blackness; the dominant group was symbolically dependent on a culture it sought to dominate.

If domination is the hub and pride of whiteness—it united under the banner of white supremacy many poor whites in the hoods of the Ku Klux Klan and sophisticated scholars in the hoods of academe—there are more spokes radiating from its center. There is whiteness standing in proxy for the blackness it helped to limit and distort. White people assumed the right to speak for the blacks they had silenced or subdued. At other times, they vainly represented the images of a people whose history and culture they had perverted through stereotype and hearsay. In important ways, this mode of whiteness parallels Renato Rosaldo's description of imperialist nostalgia, where a colonial power destroys a culture only to lament its demise with colonialism's victims.[6] Instead of nostalgia, whites presumptuously articulated the will and woes of a minority whose voices they had muffled. Needless to say, what was spoken by whites was often feeble, distorted, or idealized—the inevitable results of a colonized view of black life.

There is, too, whiteness conceived as the false victim of black power. This way of being white preserves power by protesting its loss to the real victims of white pride and power. In earlier times, the process was driven as much by the need to rally white interests as by the need to combat the exaggerated threat of black power. Whites were able to make themselves appear less powerful than they were by overstating the harm posed by blacks. D. W. Griffith's 1915 film, *Birth of a Nation*, crudely overstated black male threats to white women in order to justify the lynching of black men and to increase membership in white hate groups like the White Knights of Columbus. In our day, it is not uncommon to hear "angry white males" complain about unfair minority access to education and employment as they overstate minority success in these areas.

It is no small irony that identity politics were denounced as soon as race was debunked as a social myth. And once racial stereotypes were toppled, it made sense to challenge romantic views of minority identity. It is unsurprising that identity politics, political correctness, and multi-culturalism came under attack just as minorities gained greater say-so in the culture. It is a good thing to forcefully criticize insular or fascist identity politics. But it is intellectually irresponsible to renounce all forms of group solidarity. It is politically self-serving to damn black pride while slighting the histories and struggles that make it necessary.

Of course, taking history and struggle into account is no guarantee that the political outcome will be just. Many critics have sharply attacked the advocates of identity politics for bringing strife to the academy and the left.[7] On this view, the left—including civil rights groups, feminists, gays and lesbians, and elements of the labor movement—has blown any chance progressives have of positively impacting the culture. The Hobbesian war of all against all—pitting minority groups against the majority, blacks against whites, gays against straights, and the other-abled against the able-bodied—results in one group talking (or, more likely, hollering) past the other. All that is left are destructive politics that trade on ideological purity. Identity politics are tragic to such critics because they tarnish a history of left universalism even as they fuel needless cultural battles. The larger tragedy is that the right, long identified with privileged interests, increases its political appeal by claiming to defend the common good.

Like these critics, I deplore the sort of identity politics that unfold without concern for the common good.[8] I, too, lament the petty infighting and shameless competition for victim status among various groups. Still, such analyses don't explain how we got into the mess of identity politics to begin with. Many critics of identity politics fail to grapple with the history and social advantages of whiteness. These critics ignore how the beneficiaries of whiteness often frown on identities that fall outside their realm. They also fail to admit that the definition of universality and commonality on which left solidarity hinges is depressingly narrow. To paraphrase Alasdair MacIntyre, "Whose universality and which commonality?"

But if such critics' efforts at explicating our national malaise fall short, Michael Tomasky's similar story, rooted in the unconscious reflexes of white pride, falls far shorter.[9] In trying to figure out where the left has gone wrong, Tomasky is even more unrelenting in assailing the left's "identity politics, and how those [intellectual] underpinnings fit and don't fit the notions about a civil society that most Americans can support." According to Tomasky, "the left has completely lost touch with the regular needs of regular Americans." He contends that the left "is best described as tribal, and we're engaged in what essentially has been reduced to a battle of interest-group tribalism." Further, Tomasky claims that "solidarity based on race or ethnicity or any other such category always produces war, factionalism, fundamentalism." He concludes that "[p]articularist, interest-group politics—politics where we don't show potential allies how they benefit from being on our side—is a sure loser." Tomasky warns that it "will never do the left any good, for example, to remonstrate against angry white men." Tomasky says that this "is not to say angry white men don't exist. But what's the use in carrying on about them?"

Tomasky is right to criticize the left for its failure to show possible fellow travelers how they might be helped by tossing in with our project. And he's within reason to decry the destructive tribalism of the left. He fails, however, to understand that creating a civil society that inspires the support of most Americans cannot be the only goal of the left. The role of a marginalized but morally energized American left is also to counter the sort of injustice that passes for common sense. The welfare debate is but one example of how the left should gird its loins to defend those who are unjustly stigmatized by the advocates of universal values and common sense. Tomasky's lack of balanced historical judgment is clearly seen in his dismissal of the political and social effect of "angry white men." Tomasky underestimates how such anger often grows from the historical amnesia encouraged by white pride and by neoliberals who seek to avoid race as well.

Tomasky, and other critics of his ilk, are, to varying degrees, victims of what I term *whitewishing*. In my theory, whitewishing is an interpretation of social history where truth is synonymous with whiteness in the guise of a universal identity. Whitewishing draws equally from Freud and Feuerbach; it is the fulfillment of a fantasy of whiteness as neutral and objective. Whitewishers who embrace the myth of white universality believe they are protected from identity politics, especially since they are willing to deny their own identity politics. Whitewishing thrives on a paradox: it is both nostalgic and eschatological, driven at once by selective memories of a golden past and hopes for a perfect future where identity politics no longer prevail. This blissful state of affairs reflects a mythic past, one where minorities weren't nearly as prominent as they are now, when the left was free of the bitter divisions such groups bring.

Tomasky's and other critics' whitewishing permits them to play down three important facts. First, identity politics has always been the name of the racial and political game played in American culture. Second, white pride has played a big role in assuaging inferiority feelings in working-class whites, most of whom derived psychic consolation from not being black. Third, not all identity politics are created equal. The demand by blacks for compensatory justice in affirmative action is not special-interest pleading. It is a call to recognize that racial identity has long been the basis for conferring and denying opportunity and fairness.

Perhaps the greatest damage of white pride flares in the black psyche when black folk spurn self-respect and sadly embrace a seductive self-loathing. White pride is most effective when it finds expression in black voices. There is a truth that is often too painful to confess in public, especially around those who might exploit the information for their gain, but it is true nonetheless: Many blacks still think, as wizened blacks sometimes say, that "white water is wetter." In other words, many blacks feel that white folk possess a magic that we black folk woefully lack. This is the abysmal opposite of black pride; it is the belief in white superiority. In such a view, white money is better than black money, white authority too, and white intelligence is superior to ours. This ugly reality leaps up in all sorts of nasty ways. Sportswriter Stephen Smith bravely wrote about it when he discussed how many black basketball players routinely take their black coaches for granted. They pay deference to white coaches while defying their black ones. Smith's comments were printed, ironically enough, in 2004 on the very day that it was announced that Philadelphia 76ers head coach Randy Ayers, a black man, had been fired. A large reason behind Ayer's firing, and his failure to ignite his teams' success, may have been the unwillingness of black players to give him his just due—respect, recognition, and hard work.

But this is not a phenomenon that is limited to the hardwood floor. I have faced my share of black students in the classroom who seemed to have cognitive dissonance when a black professor held forth. This is not true of most black students, but I have had my encounter with enough to believe that my anecdotal experiences have been duplicated across the country. In fact, I recently faced a couple of belligerent students who acted out in my course at the University of Pennsylvania on the slain rapper Tupac Shakur. (It is not hard to imagine an immediate response from the cultural elite who might ask what else one expects when teaching classes on subjects that don't fit neatly into the Western canon. Since I do not believe that white intelligence or culture is inherently superior, I treat my culture, including its popular varieties, with the respect, and rigorous and critical investigation, it deserves.) During the semester, two black female students offered snide comments in class, were at times blatantly disrespectful, and, on the midterm examination blue booklet, on the line reserved for the professor's name, supplied this colorful moniker: "Michael Eric Dyson, Academic Minstrel."[10] And then, one of them flashed me the bird in a clearly sketched rendering of a middle finger after poorly answering one of the questions.

When one of the students was finally questioned in a mediation session by a black professor as to the source of her angst, she simply said that I wasn't a "real black man." I have received a great deal of criticism over the years, but the claim that I am not a "real black man" has never been made. The evidence of my inauthenticity consisted of white students signing up for my courses because they thought I was smart, and they loved to hear me talk. (I suppose if I was inarticulate and boring, I'd be "real." Such a conclusion is supported by racist logic). This angered the two black female students. On the surface, this appears to be a case of two black women gone haywire. But what it proved to me is that I wasn't given the same respect a white colleague would be shown. As I told the students, they wouldn't dare treat a white professor so rudely, not with the expectation of getting away with such behavior. (It is also doubtful that many white professors would go to the lengths I did just to get to the bottom of their problems instead of simply booting them out of class, which eventually happened to one of the students). There is a large irony involved here, one that testifies to the virulent presence of white pride in black mouths, and one not lost on most of the other black students in my class (a large one of more than two hundred students that was marvelously multiracial), one of whom summed it up nicely: "We beg for a black professor, and when we get one, we don't show him proper respect."

The belief that "white water is wetter" leads black folk to avoid supporting one another in our endeavors, as sports agents—"the white boy can get you more money" many athletes conclude, not realizing if they were to patronize the black agent, she would have more clout—as real estate brokers, as financial advisors, as limo drivers, as housekeepers, as teachers, as coaches, and sometimes, as lovers and mates. Behind that belief is a profound distrust in each other, one fed, to be sure, by a culture that in countless and subtle ways depends on that distrust. The fundamental challenge is to overcome the enticements of white pride. We must embrace a healthy self-respect that is at once self-critical and black-affirming and that encourages us to freely and bravely explore our complex humanity.

The Negro will only be free when he reaches down to the inner depths of his own being and signs with the pen and ink of assertive manhood his own emancipation proclamation. And, with a spirit straining toward true self-esteem, the Negro must boldly throw off the manacles of self-abnegation and say to himself and to the world, 'I am somebody. I am a person. I am a man with dignity and honor. I have a rich and noble history. How painful and exploited that history has been. . . . Yes, we must stand up and say, "I'm black and I'm beautiful," and this self-affirmation is the black man's need, made compelling by the white man's crimes against him.

—Martin Luther King Jr.,
"The President's Address to the
Tenth Anniversary Convention
(of the SCLC)"

CHAPTER FOUR

I Am Somebody:
Black Pride

From the time black folk arrived in the West, our bodies and minds have been under assault from one form or another of white pride. White supremacy has been a hateful myth that has unleashed untold suffering on black life. The struggle to free black folk from slavery, colonialism, and apartheid has fueled the fight for black self-respect. This fight has ranged from the 1600s to the new millennium, from slave quarters to corporate suites, from plantations to postindustrial city streets, and from Africa to America and beyond. Whether attempting to salve the wounds of the overseer's lash, or to heal the brutal psychic scars left on maturing minds, black folk have clung to pride in self as both existential armor and political weapon. Aristotle's "proper pride" could not be more necessary for a people taught to despise their flesh and to doubt their minds—and to question their souls as the conduit of divine salvation.

The need for black pride, therefore, is really quite simple: to tap the healing self-love that any group should take for granted as its birthright. White pride has often deprived blacks of the belief that they are even worthy of such love. White pride has also stymied appreciation of the intellectual and moral beauty of black life at its best. Black pride in its most rudimentary form is the soul-affirming embrace of the gifts and graces of blackness in all the ways we need for our survival. Though it seems ethically redundant to say so, black pride is steeped in a self-criticism that opens to wider avenues of racial self-discovery, and ultimately, self-respect. Black pride must be used to combat black self-hate, but it must not be confused with pride in all black things, especially those features of our existence that cramp our moral instincts or smudge our political identities.[1]

For example, one of the most troubled arenas where black pride is tested is on the skin of black folk. I recently got a reminder of how some black folk are still bewitched by skin color. "Dr. Dyson, your pictures don't do you justice," an attractive older black woman commented to me before I gave the keynote address at an educational convention. "You are much *lighter* in person." Her compliment felt like a cudgel. Though she intended to praise me, it wasn't because of anything I had done. It was only because I managed to pass what was once widely known in black communities as the "paper bag test": anyone darker than a typical sack was often ridiculed and ostracized. To be sure, these rituals of restriction were largely informal. Still, most blacks knew which groups took pride in their fair skin and straight hair, or as it used to be said, in being "light, bright, and almost white."

On another level, the older black woman's preference for my "type" marked a definite generational and gender divide. When I was a child in the 1960s, I received my share of approving glances because of my curly-but-not-kinky "good" hair and "high-yellow" skin. That preference showed up in our idols as well. Sidney Poitier was certainly admired and respected, but women swooned over the lighter Harry Belafonte. Paul Robeson's manly courage may have emitted a sober sensuality, but Adam Clayton Powell's derring-do, highlighted by a flick of his jet-black ruler-straight mane, radiated sexuality in the extreme. Things were pretty much the same for black women. Pearl Bailey's prettiness and charisma flowed freely in her multiple talents, but Lena Horne's transfixing beauty derived in part from possessing "the look." And Dorothy Dandridge outpaced all competition by lending even greater *Sturm und Drang* to the "tragic mulatto." What was viewed as attractive among blacks almost always referred to an ideal that was shaped in Europe more than in Africa.

Some of this began to change when I came of age. The civil rights movement struggled mightily to free black bodies. In too many cases, however, the mind was fettered in what may be inelegantly termed white worship, or at least "light" worship. But there were glimmers of real hope. As a teen in the seventies, black pride locked my curls into an afro. And I draped dashikis over my amber limbs. But my light-skinned look was still almost automatically "in." Even black men who espoused nationalist sentiment seemed to prefer a light-skinned sister when they couldn't seduce a white woman. (The rationale for such interracial dalliances was often amusing. As one nationalist explained his miscegenating behavior to a prominent civil rights leader, "I'm punishing her father"). "Black is beautiful" may have been a powerful slogan, but it wasn't until quite recently that we began to appreciate our kinky hair, broad noses, big lips, and dark skin.

But even now qualifications must be made. The chocolate charm of darker brothers is now the rage in some black communities and beyond. As my then twenty-two-year-old son explained to me a few years back, "Dad, us light-skinned guys aren't in anymore; the girls love the dark brothers." It's true that actor Wesley Snipes is a sculpted sex symbol. Tyson Beckford's modeling career is chiseled from his Afro-Asiatic features. Singer D'Angelo is a roughneck romantic whose appeal ripples through his bronze biceps. And grown women lose control in the glare of Denzel Washington's impishly iridescent smile. But many younger black men, like many of their elders, still seem to be color-struck. Certainly actresses Angela Bassett and Gabrielle Union may strike their fancy. But the acid test is really on their arms and in their fantasies, at least as far as such fantasies can be detected in the near ubiquitous music videos that reflect and urge on the hip-hop generation. Light-skinned and "exotic" Asian- or Latino-looking black women flood the visual landscape of the adolescent and adult male. While young black females seem to have a weakness for chocolate, many young males prefer vanilla.

Of course, such preferences can never be simply read as the expression of self-loathing or the attempt to escape *obvious* blackness, although both options are too often true. I can remember the confusion I felt when some kid would say to me, "You think you're cute 'cause you're light-skinned" when nothing was farther from my mind. But I wasn't consoled by recognizing that sometimes my peers projected onto me their anxiety about the skin hierarchy that ruled our roosts. I learned enough to know that we can never assume that righteousness resides in dark skin, a point illuminated by Clarence Thomas's career. Neither can we conclude that light skin eradicates authenticity or courage, a notion that Malcolm X's life clearly challenges. But as I told the educational convention where I received my dubious compliments, I know that I gain access to certain audiences because of how I "look." The trick is to become a Trojan Horse: I, and those like me, must smuggle in visions of identity that challenge the inflexible images that patrol the borders of blackness. We must resist the seductive rewards of white pride in black skin.

One of the most deceptive uses of black pride is glimpsed when conservatives argue that black folk should be proud of black achievement no matter its political pedigree or consequence. Hence, black pride is manipulated to bully black folk into accepting ideas and personalities that are hostile to our interests. This underside to black pride—conjuring racial fellow feeling because folk belong to the same race—is often deemed a vice by those who seem to forget that lesson when it works to their advantage. The same conservative folk usually criticize black folk who rally to common racial interests. At times, however, conservatives say that black pride is the reason we should embrace blacks who are uncomfortable with the notion that black pride should determine political allegiance.

The manipulation of black pride by quarters that usually shy away from such matters was clearly glimpsed in 2001 when George W. Bush nominated Colin Powell as secretary of state, Condoleezza Rice as national security adviser, and Rod Paige as secretary of education. His advocates argued that his nominations proved that Bush was serious about racial diversity. Moreover, Bush's nominations of a Latino and two white women to his cabinet suggested that compassionate conservatism boasted enough room for all sorts of minorities. But conservatives seemed to be saying to black folk who were critical of Bush's racial politics that we should be proud of Powell, Rice, and Paige because "one of us" was working prominently for "one of them." By playing the pride card, conservatives hoped to reshuffle the racial deck and thus put blacks on the defensive by denying that we were incidental to the Republican Party. Here were three figures that all blacks should be proud of to represent "us" in the conservative political mainstream. Here, of course, is where the urge for black pride can career out of control. Sometimes the need for black faces in high places blinds us to the fact that the moral substance of one's identity is more important than pigment.

At base, political complexion is more critical than shade of face; ideological hue is more valuable than tint of skin. To be proud of Powell, Rice, or Paige because their skin is black distorts the morality of black pride, which promotes the uplift of black culture and celebrates the complex features of black identity. History and politics shape the racial solidarity on which black pride rests. Such solidarity must be continually redefined by the black folk who bind together in pursuit of common interests. Not all blacks will see things in the same light. Our competing interests and alternative beliefs spring from the growth of black culture beyond comfortable ideological boundaries. This doesn't mean that black pride can't exist for all blacks. It simply means that the same sorts of black pride cannot be reasonably expected to exist in all blacks. What might cause a black conservative to feel pride in Powell or Rice might cause other blacks shame and disgust. Some blacks who oppose Rice or Powell on ideological grounds may feel twinges of pride for their intelligence, perseverance, and character. Such pride, however, must never trump moral truth in favor of racial tribalism.

The nominations of Powell, Rice, and Paige were instructive. Black folk had serious doubts about their devotion to the interests of the people they were supposed to make proud. These doubts far outweighed the benefits of hoisting the trio on our collective shoulders. Powell's nomination took little imagination or courage. For Bush to take credit for nominating a national hero to extend his stellar record of public service was only a little better than Al Gore taking credit for inventing the Internet. There was great hope that Powell's halo effect would redound to Bush. But his choice of Powell owed nothing to Bush's fundamental bearing as a racial statesman. Powell and Bush were at significant odds on crucial issues. Powell's vigorous support of affirmative action, his belief in a woman's right to choose, and his advocacy for besieged urban children put him to the left of the Bush dogma. To be sure, Powell was no radical. His moderate racial principles were tolerable to many blacks because they didn't seem all that bad for a man who stood in the Republican camp. The same couldn't be said for Congressman J. C. Watts, the black Republican former congressman from Oklahoma whose politics were aggressively conservative. Powell's beliefs ran the same blush of racial centrism that flowed through the Clinton administration over its eight-year neoliberal run. The difference is that such moderates, and a sprinkling of liberals, had plenty of company in the Clinton administration. In Bush's administration, Powell was definitely an odd man out.

Neither did Powell's beliefs have a substantive impact on Bush's domestic policies that hampered black progress. What looked like a plum for black folk was in many ways a political pit. True, no black person before Powell had ever served as secretary of state. But pride in Powell's achievement offered little solace to blacks who bore the weight of Bush's tax cuts for the wealthy or his slashing of social and educational programs for the poor. Indeed, Powell had not been nominated as secretary of Health and Human Services, where his input on welfare reform might have been useful.

Since Powell's training did not prepare him to serve as attorney general, he could not choose the civil rights czar who sets racial policy from the Justice Department. Instead, that honor fell to John Ashcroft, an ultraconservative whose opposition to black interests was destructive. An omen of things to come was starkly glimpsed in Ashcroft's contemptuous scuttling of the nomination of black Missouri Supreme Court Justice Ronnie White for the federal bench. Powell's value to Bush on race was largely symbolic. Moreover, Powell's racial symbolism was exploited to provide cover for policies that harmed the overwhelming majority of black Americans who were never persuaded by Powell to join the party of Lincoln. (Who can forget Bush's assault on affirmative action on Martin Luther King Jr.'s birthday in 2003? It proved the limited value of pride in conservative black appointees who couldn't keep their boss from opposing a policy that Powell strongly supported, but one that Rice barely did. Rice's stance suggests, too, how futile it is to be proud of black folk who oppose the values and interests of most blacks.)

Rice and Paige were at the time lesser-known political quantities, but their nominations nonetheless revealed Bush's racial politics. Rice, the former Stanford provost and assistant national security adviser for President George H. W. Bush, was not a vocal supporter of affirmative action, preferring a lukewarm version of the policy that fused with Bush's nebulous substitute for the policy, "affirmative access." At Stanford, Rice

was not nearly as aggressive as she might reasonably have been in recruit-
ing black faculty, failing to match the efforts of her colleagues at equally
conservative universities like Duke. And her record of advising the se-
nior Bush on national security matters indicates that she was a blue-
blood conservative in blackface.

As for Paige, his my-way-or-the-highway methods yielded mixed
results for the predominantly black and Latino students in Houston,
where he served six years as superintendent of schools. A proponent of
annual standardized tests, a measure heartily supported by Bush, Paige
oversaw rising test scores while all but abandoning students who couldn't
pass muster. Moreover, Paige supported the use of tax money to fund
private education, a policy favored by Bush and many blacks but that has
had negative effects on poor families. The lure of vouchers is seductive,
but their advocates ignore how there is hardly enough money to make a
real difference to those students whose parents are financially strapped.

With Rice's nomination as national security adviser—four years
before her spectacular rise as the first black female secretary of state—the
right seemed to be saying that a black woman could be just as staunch in
spouting conservative foreign policy as the next wonk. With Paige, the
point seemed to be that a black man could promote the sort of educational policies that help some black folk while harming a larger segment
of the community. ("Leave No Child Behind," a phrase pinched from
Marian Wright Edelman's Children's Defense Fund and initiated under
Paige's watch before his departure as education secretary, did just the

opposite, leaving behind millions of poor, black, and brown students). It is clear that proclaiming black pride in figures whose efforts significantly undermine black progress is neither healthy nor productive. The irony is that Powell, Paige, and Rice were chosen in part to prove an inclusiveness that turned out to be relatively meaningless. Their presence in the Bush administration came at the expense of not representing the interests of the majority of blacks, especially poor and working-class folk who are vulnerable and largely invisible. The lesson the Republicans would have us learn from Powell's, Rice's, and Paige's posts is that not all blacks think alike, that we represent no ideological monolith in liberal captivity. The real lesson may be that a black face does not automatically translate into a progressive political presence that aids the bulk of black folk. Especially when that face must put a smile on repressive policies that hurt most blacks and other Americans committed to radical democracy.

At another extreme is the expectation that black folk will take pride in those blacks who were born to, or have managed to crawl into, the black elite. Even as they rank on blacks from lesser stations, the black elite expect the admiration of the very blacks they dismiss, while seeking acclaim from their own set. If being proud of black conservatives who undermine black interests is troubling, it is an act of self-hatred to take pride in those who take pride in putting down ordinary black folk. I got a sense of this several years ago when I was invited to address a local New Jersey meeting of Jack and Jill, a social organization that helps the kids of the black upper crust to network and enhance their own privileged identities. I figured they had made a big mistake, since I was a lifelong member of the unelite. In fact, I had a special disdain for their ilk since growing up in a working-class Detroit family and being taunted by some Jack and Jill members for my visible lack of credentials. The fact that my first girlfriend's father was largely responsible for me attending a prestigious boarding school in one of Detroit's toniest suburbs meant little to highfalutin' Negroes, especially since I was kicked out after a year—only to return to Detroit to become a teen father who went on welfare and didn't make it to college until age twenty-one.

The New Jersey Jack and Jill event was an authors' tea where several writers discussed their work. When it came time for me to stand and deliver, I devilishly drew on my reserves of refined resentment, intending to score a few points for the brothers and sisters who would never penetrate such circles. "I write about, think about, criticize, and feel closest to *niggas*," I said. My audience was temporarily stunned to silence. "I don't mean *niggers*, the term of derision employed by white folk; I mean *niggas*, those black folk who fall under the judgmental, moralizing scrutiny of elite blacks who think that there's an essential, ontological difference between rich blacks and the rest of black Americans." To complete my mission, I made what to many of my hearers was a startling confession. "I guess I write so much about *niggas* because, as I've been reminded most of my life, I am one."

That scene flashed through my mind as I read about the black elite, especially in Lawrence Otis Graham's *Our Kind of People*, which is a revealing, occasionally riveting, and finally repulsive book, mostly because it celebrates the enduring class bigotries of the black elite that I attempted to boil off at the authors' tea, and later in my book *Is Bill Cosby Right? Or Has the Black Middle Class Lost Its Mind?*[2] Fortunately, the New Jersey folk proved to be much more pliable and self-critical than the groups Graham details. By the end of my talk, they even laughed out loud at my suggestion that they change the name of the group to "Rasheed and Shaniqua" to reflect working-class culture, and in so doing, challenged my views about their uniform snobbery. But readers of Graham's book will find little criticism of the pathological materialism, exaggerated self-importance, and the nearly unbridled keeping-up-with-the-Joneses that pervade black elite subcultures. Of course, even before the vicious but true portrait that sociologist E. Franklin Frazier painted in his classic *Black Bourgeoisie*—a world teeming with destructive careerism and self-hating rituals—the stereotype of the black hoi polloi as self-serving wannabes persisted. *Our Kind of People* only reinforces this perception.

To be fair, Graham's insider look at the black elite contains a huge, winning feature: it is the first extended examination by one of their own, as Graham drops major science about the mating habits (always rich), skin preference (always light), and hair ideal (always straight) of the black ruling class. While not formal social science, it is nonetheless a poignant, informal ethnography of a large swath of black America that only occasionally rises to visibility in our culture, as it did when *The Cosby Show* ruled the ratings and caused controversy because a whole lot of folk—including blacks—refused to believe that such a family could exist. True enough, the implicit raison d'être for Graham's book is the ridiculous belief that black culture and its representations are exhausted by stereotypical views of black ghetto life. But two wrongs don't give black elites the right to dismiss and disparage their lesser kin. *Our Kind of People* is full of bile and bluster, as the black elite speak for themselves in the more than three hundred interviews that Graham conducted for his book.

What Graham's book does like no other is copiously detail the likes and dislikes, the sins and secret ceremonies, but especially the mixed virtues (they give lots of money to black causes as checkbook activists, they fight racial injustice against the *black rich*) and many vices (they hate poor blacks, they look down on middle-class blacks, they are relentlessly materialistic and snobbish) of the privileged few. And on occasion Graham manages to gently score the black elite for their bad faith. He calls black Episcopalians and Congregationalists "cynical and status-conscious" when they chose those churches "simply because most blacks were not of that faith." To his credit, Graham tells of all the good work that black female organizations (such as the Links, the Girl Friends, the Drifters, and sororities like Alpha Kappa Alpha and Delta Sigma Theta) and black male groups (such as the Boulé, the National Association of Guardsmen, One Hundred Black Men, and fraternities like Alpha Phi Alpha and Omega Psi Phi) do for less-advantaged black folk; things such as voter drives, inner-city mentoring projects, and tutoring black youth. But that's hardly enough to inspire pride in their achievements, especially since those achievements are often undermined by troubling assaults on poor blacks.

Graham's portrait is unintentionally damning, since he fails to see that too often the black elite are just as nefarious in the minds of the black masses as white racist elites are in the lives of the black upper crust. Most of the groups Graham details can be entered only through nomination by existing members, an incestuous practice that polices pedigree with wanton zeal. The tragedy is that Graham fails to get how ultimately bad that is. He was full of bitter irony when it came to posing as a waiter in an all-white country club that looked down on blacks, a story he told in his insightful book *Member of the Club*.[3] He has none of that irony as he allows us to grab a glimpse of an equally cloistered world full of ambition and arrogance toward the black masses from whom they seek a safe distance.

Throughout his book we find statements like the following from a San Francisco member of the Links: "Maybe it sounds a little pretentious, but I simply can't waste time getting to know women who aren't Links. It's an automatic screen that lets me know this person comes from the right background and has the same values. I'm almost fifty and I live a busy life. I don't have time for people who don't have the right stuff. Rich, educated white women don't hang around with middle-class college dropouts, so why should I?" That very well states the barely suppressed premise of Graham's book: rich black folk can be every bit as coy, sophisticated, snobbish, high-handed, mean-spirited, self-concerned, and pretentious as rich white folk. And hence the danger of seeing racial progress in terms of its density of replication: if we can make black communities more like white communities—with the caveat that we can bemoan white racism but rarely decry black elitism—then the world will be all right. To take pride in such a vicious practice would justifiably invite the charge of self-hatred.

In the end, Graham is too little the black elite's critic and altogether its obsequious chronicler. Throughout this tendentious *apologia pro vita elite*, Graham flings toadies to the high-toned hypocrites who mock the virtues of hard work, academic achievement, and social standing by believing only they possess the right ingredients for success. This attitude is constantly displayed by Graham, as he, for instance, decries the egalitarianism that some Jack and Jill members seek to unleash on the group, confessing that "a part of me recoiled at the suggestion that the group could or should be more diverse or open-minded. . . . I wasn't sure I wanted one of its members suggesting that it was changing or even *needed* to change." There's no doubt that African America is a differentiated group—hardly the picture of pathology or self-destruction that passes for common sense in the monolithic versions of black culture that fly in some scholarly circles and soar on the small screen. The irony is that there is plenty of self-destruction and pathology in a book attempting to rebut such stereotypes of black life. Surely black life is wider than the narrow choices of either ghettocentric authenticity or rituals of ruthless upward climbing.

The search for alternatives to either extreme is what motivates black pride—or black shame and disgust, or sometimes a mixture of them all—in the artists who carry the burden of representing the race on screen. When such artists are rewarded with the highest recognition of their peers, black pride raises several decibels higher. This is true even when the images created by those who are saluted are complex, problematic, or the cause of no small racial wincing, often all at the same time. Such was the case when Halle Berry and Denzel Washington were showered with Oscars in 2002 for their roles, respectively, as a desperate woman seeking sexual and spiritual relief from existential horror in trysts with a racist partner, and as a rogue cop whose ethical impoverishment was matched by the stylish debauchery with which he pursued his fiendish appetites. But the acceptance of the Oscars by Berry and Washington marked a high moment of black pride.

As Halle Berry strode to the podium to accept her best-actress Oscar, the first for a black woman, she wept uncontrollably and gasped, "This moment is so much bigger than me." Just as revealing was Denzel Washington's resolute dispassion as he accepted his best-actor Oscar, only the second for a black man, by glancing at the trophy and uttering through a half-smile, "Two birds in one night, huh?" Their contrasting styles—one explicit, the other implied—say a great deal about the burdens of representing the race in Hollywood. Berry electrified her audience, speaking with intelligence and rousing emotion of how her Oscar was made possible by the legendary likes of Dorothy Dandridge, Lena Horne, and

Diahann Carroll. And in a stunning display of sorority in a profession riven by infighting and narcissism, Berry acknowledged the efforts of contemporary black actresses Angela Bassett, Jada Pinkett Smith, and Vivica Fox. But it was when Berry moved from ancestors and peers to the future that she spoke directly to her award's symbolic meaning. She gave the millions who watched around the globe not only a sorely needed history lesson but instruction as well in courageously identifying with the masses. Berry tearfully declared that her award was for "every nameless, faceless woman of color" who now has a chance, since "this door has been opened." Black pride couldn't have found a more eloquent voice.

Berry's courage and candor are depressingly rare among famed blacks with a lot on the line: money, prestige, reputation, and work. Many covet the limelight's payoffs but cower at its demands. Even fewer speak up about the experiences their ordinary brothers and sisters endure—and if they are honest, that they themselves too often confront—on a daily basis. To be sure, there is an unspoken tariff on honesty among the black privileged: If they dare go against the grain, they may be curtailed in their efforts to succeed or be cut off from the rewards they deserve. Or they may endure stigma. Think of the huge controversy over basketball great Charles Barkley's comments near the time of the 2002 Oscars that racism haunts golf, that everyday black folk still fight bigotry, and that black athletes are too scared to speak up, which is the common banter of most blacks. What Berry did was every bit as brave. Her achievement, she insisted, was now the hope of anonymous women of color around the globe. Berry proved that on such occasions, black pride's payoff is the shining and unapologetic representation of the aspirations of ordinary people to do extraordinary deeds.

At first blush, it may seem that Denzel Washington failed to stand up and "represent." But that would be a severe misreading of the politics of signifying that thread through black culture. Looking up to the balcony where Sidney Poitier sat—having received an honorary Oscar earlier before delivering a stately speech—Washington said, "Forty years I've been chasing Sidney. . . ." He joked with Poitier, and the academy, by playfully lamenting his being awarded an Oscar on the same night that his idol was feted. Washington, for a fleeting but telling moment, transformed the arena of his award into an intimate platform of conversation between himself and his progenitor that suggested, "This belongs to us, we are not interlopers, nobody else matters more than we do." Thus, Washington never let us see him sweat, behaving as if it was natural, if delayed, that he should receive the highest recognition of his profession. His style, the complete opposite of Berry's, was political in the way that only black cool can be when the stakes are high and its temperature must remain low, sometimes beneath the detection of the powers-that-be that can stamp it out. This is not to be confused with spineless selling out. Nor is it to be seen as yielding to the cowardly imperative to keep one's mouth shut in order to hang on to one's privilege. Rather, it is the strategy of those who break down barriers and allow the chroniclers of their brokenness to note their fall.

Both approaches—we can call them conscience and cool—are vital, especially if Hollywood is to change. Conscience informs and inspires. It tells the film industry we need more producers, directors, writers, and executives who can greenlight projects by people of color. It also reminds the black blessed of their obligation to struggle onscreen and off for justice. Cool prepares and performs. It pays attention to the details of great art and exercises its craft vigorously as opportunity allows, thus paving the way for more opportunities. The fusion of both approaches is nicely summed up in a lyric by James Brown: "I don't want nobody to give me nothin' / Just open up the door, I'll get it myself."

Brown's phrase—the ultimate expression of pride in doing for oneself, an often forgotten dimension of black pride—shines through in numerous tales of rising from want to high achievement, highlighting the joy taken in working hard and the equally necessary effort of removing barriers that prevent others from doing the same. Thus, the ultimate end of black pride is to replicate itself, to provide the conditions of success for those who follow behind, and who follow through. In such cases, the lives of those who overcome, rise up, and "get over" merit admiration because they are moral examples of the excellence and incentive that pride produces.

Kweisi Mfume is an individual we can, and should, admire. His life story, as told in his memoir *No Free Ride,* is in many ways a classically American one: A soul seemingly destined for failure—born poor, living on the wrong side of town, in a family with no education—interrupts his fate by rallying against misfortune and then lands on top of a world that might well have crushed him.[4] No matter how often we hear that story, no matter what hue it comes in or what heritage it reflects, our hearts cannot help but swell with pride.

Mfume was born Frizzell Gray in 1948. Dubbed "Pee Wee" by an aunt for his diminutive stature, he spent the first twelve years of his life in Turner's Station, "an all-black, blue-collar town perched quietly on the western shore of the Chesapeake Bay." From the start, however, there was trouble in this pastoral, relatively sheltered black homestead. Mfume's father terrorized the household: He withheld affection from Kweisi and his three sisters, and beat their mother, Mary. But in 1959, as Mfume stoically recalls, "my father left for work and never returned again." Already the center of his world, his mother became the reason for Mfume's strong determination to make something good of his life.

Mary's hopes for her only son would be greatly delayed by his enthusiastic embrace of the survival ethic of the tough ghetto streets of West Baltimore, where the family moved when he was twelve. When Mfume was sixteen, Mary died of cancer in her son's arms. The trauma of her death spurred a downward spiral in Mfume's life that would take the better part of a decade to reverse. Always a smart, if underachieving, student, he dropped out of high school, "working at menial jobs, living in a small room, and wasting my time. My world on its best day was a mixture of scheming, gaming, hustling, and brawling. I was going no-where fast and chasing after things that would never last." By the time he was twenty-two, he had fathered five sons out of wedlock.

By telling the story of his erratic early life, of course, Mfume is aware, and reminds us as well, of the political utility of memory, of how the past always has a future, driven in part by the reasons we have in the present to revisit, and inevitably recast, the experiences of days gone by. But the past, especially the past that swings on the hinges of personal narrative, is about more than mere events. It's also about how, and even more tellingly, why things happened as they did. Sprinkled throughout Mfume's narrative are judicious but forceful reminders of his progressive political perspective; it's clear that he's viewing the past and his own painful pilgrimage through the lens of his present commitment—at the time as the newly elected president of the NAACP—to the poor and the racially oppressed.

Thus, Mfume's narrative of personal transformation—of defeating the forces that were out to defeat him—becomes a blueprint for racial reconstruction. It is not a new concept: The belief that "my story" is a reflection of, contains important facets of, can lead to a strengthening of "our story" has been with us for a while. From Frederick Douglass's to Angela Davis's stories, the black autobiography has served as an index of individual ingenuity and moral purpose as well as a record of the race's resources for stating and then struggling toward its collective ambitions. In this light, the parts of Mfume's memoir that detail his transformation—his choice of a Ghanaian name to signify his intellectual and spiritual rebirth, his return to school for a GED and then a college degree, his student activism and work as a disc jockey, his membership in the Baltimore City Council and the U.S. Congress, where he almost single-handedly revived the Congressional Black Caucus, his position with the NAACP, and his pledge to run for the Senate—are about still another fusion: that of the American myth of individual self-reinvention and the African American myth of racial uplift.

"What was it that caused me to rise so high from ashes so deep?" he asks. And looking upon the faces of young gang members loitering on a street corner, he muses: "These kids are not beyond rescue or redemption any more than they are beyond hope or help. They are a part of the other America, trapped and lost in every big city and every small town. They are the ones we pass by in our cars as we lock our doors. They are the ones who flirt with death and test our limits. They become teenage parents much too soon, and give up on life much too fast. They are black and white and Latino. And, most of all they are real. . . . My story like theirs, is a constant reminder of the fragility of human life, and the divine power that mediates the war between success and failure."

As Mfume proves in his eloquently rendered and always moving memoir, he is too canny to surrender the terrain of American myth and American heroism to the likes of John Wayne or Ronald Reagan. Mfume knows that black folk deserve a seat at the table of larger-than-life figures as well, precisely because they've taken personal responsibility for bettering themselves in a society that is ugly and intransigent. But he is too wise and weathered to ignore the lethal limits imposed on those whose skin is black, whose station is low, and whose starting place in life is compromised by a legacy of inequality. Mfume knows that self-help makes sense only when the selves black folk work valiantly to fashion can count on the opportunity and justice their land promises all its citizens. *No Free Ride* proves that Henry David Thoreau is right: that any man more right than his neighbors, especially when those neighbors are puffed-up politicians who have benefited from social and economic supports they now seek to destroy, is a majority of one.

Black pride, whether it concerns our skin, our politics, our social order, our culture, or our stories of overcoming, is rooted in our will to be as free as possible to love ourselves without apology or regret. Black self-respect and self-esteem are impossible without an appreciation for the moral and political struggles that our best lights have waged to carve spaces of loving affirmation in the universe. We must never allow our pride to eclipse our moral purposes; nor should we allow ourselves to be manipulated by forces out to exploit black pride to subvert true black progress. Black pride is only as healthy and productive as the black people who carry its virtuous traits forward in an often hostile and senseless world. Then, too, black pride encourages identification with victims of oppression, at home, and around the world, challenging the chorus of voices that spout the unquestioning embrace of national pride.

There is no cure for the pride of a virtuous nation but pure religion. The pride of a powerful nation may be humbled by the impotence that defeat brings. The pride of a virtuous nation cannot be humbled by moral and political criticisms because in comparative terms it may actually be virtuous. The democratic traditions of the Anglo-Saxon world are actually the potential basis of a just world order. But the historical achievements of this world are full of violations and contradictions of these principles. "In God's sight" they are not just; and they know it if they place themselves under the divine scrutiny, that is, if they regard their own history prayerfully rather than comparatively and measure themselves by what is demanded of them rather than by comparing their success with the failure of others. Thus a contrite recognition of our own sins destroys the illusion of eminence through virtue and lays the foundation for the apprehension of "grace" in our national life. We know that we have the position that we hold in the world today partly by reason of factors and forces in the complex pattern of history that we did not create and from which we do not deserve to benefit. If we apprehend this religiously, the sense of destiny ceases to be a vehicle of pride and becomes the occasion for a new sense of responsibility.

—Reinhold Niebuhr,
"Anglo-Saxon Destiny and Responsibility"

My Country Right or Wrong?
National Pride

If pride should on occasion be thought of as a vice, even as a sin, it is particularly true when the subject is national pride. It is not that pride in one's nation is necessarily a vice or sin. After all, love of one's country is a healthy attribute of citizenship around the globe. It is when love turns to worship that national pride becomes a destabilizing force. Worship of national identity robs citizens of an appreciation of the country's productive role in the world beyond its own borders. Since America is the last remaining superpower, our role in the world and our view of our nation is especially influential. Nothing has underscored this more than our national self-image after the terrorist attacks of September 11, 2001.

September 11 is now lodged at the center of the American imagination. Our preoccupation reveals at once how parochial we have been—after all, other nations, and others in our nation, have suffered terror for decades—and how insecure we feel as a nation. Even as the importance of September 11 is acknowledged, we must also admit the nation's role in unleashing terror on its own citizens. September 11 is also viewed as a national touchstone to define authentic American citizenship. Unfortunately, other equally significant dates in the nation's history, especially for citizens of color, are overlooked or excluded. As educational theorist Gloria Ladson-Billings argues:

> Over and over people in this country describe the world as pre–September 11 and post–September 11. Yes, this is a significant date, for now, but it takes history to determine whether or not it will become a teleological fault line. For me time and chronology can be divided in an infinite number of combinations: pre–April 4, 1968 (assassination of MLK) and post–April 4, 1968, pre–summer of 1963 and post–summer of 1963 (bombing of the little girls in the Birmingham church), pre–summer of 1955 and post–summer of 1955 (murder of Emmett Till). Each of these events made *me* feel less safe, less secure, less able to lay claim to any notion of myself as American. But, now I am learning that September 11 is the dividing line I must use if I am ever to claim

"real" citizenship. All other notions of what is or is not important become subjugated to this new indicator that is reinscribed in every newspaper, every broadcast, and every popular media outlet.[1]

Ladson-Billings also points out that the claim that America will "never be the same" after the September 11 terrorist attacks denies how we have tragically conducted political business as usual. The nation quickly adopted rhetoric "about the need to place Americans of Arab/Middle Eastern descent under strict surveillance and to restrict their freedom," and entertained "a number of proposals aimed at curtailing civil liberties—military tribunals instead of civilian courts, restricting access to presidential papers, coercion of national loyalty."[2] Ladson-Billings suggests that these efforts "reflect not how we are different, but rather how easily we retreat to old patterns of behaviors and old discourse that almost always lead to bad results. The same kinds of responses were apparent after Pearl Harbor."[3] As Ladson-Billings explains, the September 11 attacks have only increased the difficulty of arguing about what constitutes genuine American identity, narrowing the range of options on the table.

> The difficult issue is that we are more likely to be exactly like we were (and even more so, if that is possible) because of September 11. Before the attack, the very concept of an American was being contested. It was a fluid concept that was being made and remade in a myriad of ways. In some places it included a variety

of language groups–English, Spanish, French Creole, Vietnamese, Hmong. In other places it included a variety of religious practices. In still other places it included race, class, gender, sexuality, and ability differences. However, it was not a settled or definitive concept. Soon after September 11 who and what constituted an American became a fixed and rigid image. And, that concept has little room for dissent or challenge. I fear there will be a retreat to nativist and parochial thinking about who we are and who or what the "other" is.[4]

The hunger to narrowly define American citizenship is only one consequence of September 11; our pervasive national unease is another. The strike on the Twin Towers and the Pentagon, symbols of America's financial and military might, underscores a vulnerability we have rarely, if ever, felt as a people. That is the bitter point of terrorism: to impose on enemies a sense of ultimate insecurity and fear that makes citizens feel confused, sad, angry, disoriented—and above all, unsafe. The combination of heightened awareness of terror and our vulnerability in its shadow can lead to a renewed sense of our solidarity with victims around the globe. It can also result in an unreasonable self-absorption that amplifies the most vicious elements of national pride. Philosopher Martha Nussbaum captures this reality when she writes:

The world has come to a stop—in a way that it never has for Americans, when disaster befalls human beings in other places.

Floods, earthquakes, cyclones—and the daily deaths of thousands from preventable malnutrition and disease—none of these typically makes the American world come to a standstill, none elicits a tremendous outpouring of grief and compassion. The plight of innocent civilians in the current war evokes a similarly uneven and flickering response.

And worse: our sense that the "us" is all that matters can easily flip over into a demonizing of an imagined "them," a group of outsiders who are imagined as enemies of the invulnerability and the pride of the all-important "us." Compassion for our fellow Americans can all too easily slide over into an attitude that wants America to come out on top, defeating or subordinating other peoples or nations. Anger at the terrorists themselves is perfectly appropriate; so is the attempt to bring them to justice. But "us-them" thinking doesn't always stay focused on the original issue; it too easily becomes a general call for American supremacy, the humiliation of "the other."[5]

But if America feels these emotions now, we must confess that we have been largely insensitive to how much of the world confronts these realities every day. We have been spared the psychic wounds that result from the arbitrary violence of subway bombings. We have been exempt from the collective sorrow that descends in the aftermath of routine physical assaults from true believers. And we have been largely protected from the bullets and bayonets wielded by marauding militia. If we have been oblivious to the world's suffering from terrorism, we are in deeper denial about the shameful role our nation has played in unjust practices around the globe. Our national pride, and the measures we have taken to defend it, has also made us terrorists to nations we have explicitly or subtly vanquished. This is no attempt to justify the terror of September 11; it is simply a reminder that America has acted in unconscionable ways toward other nations in the pursuit of our narrowly defined self-interests, including in the Middle East. The current international resentment we face as Americans grows mainly from our advocacy of colonialist and imperialist politics in the region. We must not forget that the CIA funneled millions of dollars to Afghanistan rebels who sought to rid their nation of its Soviet presence. Ironically, Osama bin Laden was aided in his unscrupulous practices by his association with the CIA, one of our government's most notorious agencies.

Unfortunately, America has often been incapable of distinguishing its valiant role in opposing injustice on one shore from its vicious role in extending it in other theaters. As Christian theologian Reinhold Niebuhr reminded the nation in the aftermath of its just role in World War II in opposing Nazi Germany and imperial Japan:

> We were indeed the executors of God's judgment yesterday. But we might remember the prophetic warnings to the nations of old, that nations which become proud because they were divine instruments must in turn stand under the divine judgment and be

destroyed. . . . If ever a nation needed to be reminded of the perils of vainglory, we are that nation in the pride of our power and our victory.[6]

A few years later, Niebuhr warned against General Douglas MacArthur's desire to bomb Manchuria in 1950 during the Korean War by linking the general's strategy to the vainglory he had written about earlier:

> Great nations are too strong to be destroyed by their foes. But they can easily be overcome by their own pride. One has the uneasy feeling that our own country is greatly tempted in this critical age to that pride, in which the prophets of old recognized the portent of Babylon's doom.[7]

His warnings are still relevant in our own "critical age," the Age of Terror.

Too often, the exposure of America's will to pride has been dismissed as unpatriotic. This is particularly true in our Age of Terror, when the expression of dissent—an expression that offends national pride by puncturing the tribal truths on which it feeds—is characterized as anti-American. This is a vicious ploy to suppress the critical voices that are the very lifeblood of national thriving. Without the safeguards of free speech and open debate, the prospects of democracy are doomed. The voice of the dissenter is often the conscience of the nation. Niebuhr's prophetic voice rang forth in the first half of the twentieth century; Martin Luther King Jr.'s voice was a clarion call for freedom and democracy in the century's closing half.

"God didn't call America to do what she's doing in the world now," King thundered from his Atlanta pulpit exactly two months before his death at the hands of a cowardly racial terrorist. "God didn't call America to engage in a senseless, unjust war."[8] Here, of course, King referred to the Vietnam War, and he took a lashing in public for his dissenting views. He was accused of being unpatriotic. He was charged with moral treason. Other black leaders like Roy Wilkins and Whitney Young lambasted him (though they later came to acknowledge, as did the nation, that King's views were courageous and correct). And yet, King was one of the greatest patriots this nation has produced. He proved it by giving his life in a fight to defend this country's best side against its worst. As we struggle for ethical guidance in the shadow of terrorism and war, it is good to remember that dissent helps national flourishing and aids in clarifying our political vision. If King's actions against war prove anything, it's that there's a huge difference between patriotism and nationalism.

Patriotism is the critical affirmation of one's country in light of its best values, including the attempt to correct it when it's in error. Nationalism is the uncritical support of one's nation regardless of its moral or political bearing. Patriotism derives from the word *patria*, or the noncompetitive love of one's country. It was only in the nineteenth century when a sense of competition among territories emerged through the concept of nationalism that pride in country became unpleasant and problematic.[9] In this view, patriotism "is *self-referential*" while "feelings of nationalism are inherently *comparative*—and, almost exclusively, downwardly comparative . . . [T]he patriot is noncompetitive and the nationalist competitive."[10] Finally, patriotism "often takes the form of beliefs in the *social system* and *values* of one's country. Expressions of nationalism, on the other hand, are often appeals to advance the *national interests* in the international order."[11] This latter version of an insular and narrowly conceived national pride is expressed in the slogan, "my country, right or wrong." Too often nationalism has prevailed over patriotism in expressions of national pride. The confusion between the two has blurred the difference between love and worship of country, a distinction King never failed to make.

In a commencement address at Lincoln University in 1961, King praised the American dream and the Declaration of Independence, saying that "seldom if ever in the history of the world has a sociopolitical document expressed in such profoundly eloquent and unequivocal language the dignity and the worth of human personality."[12] And when he gave his famous "I Have a Dream" speech before the Lincoln Memorial in 1963, King reaffirmed that his dream was "deeply rooted in the American dream that one day this nation will rise up and live out the true meaning of its creed: 'We hold these truths to be self-evident, that all men are created equal.'"[13]

But King understood the contradictions at the heart of American society. In his Lincoln University commencement address, King said "since the founding fathers of our nation dreamed this noble dream, America has been something of a schizophrenic personality, tragically divided against herself."[14] America, King understood, preaches democracy but practices its selective application. Moreover, King understood the perils of an isolationist nationalism that celebrates one's country at the expense of recognizing one's global citizenship. In such a case, loyalty to nation might turn vicious, demanding that one subordinate moral principle to narrow national self-interest. In his church sermon, King said that in Vietnam, America had "committed more war crimes almost than any nation in the world." And we wouldn't stop it "because of our pride and our arrogance as a nation."[15]

Earlier, in his landmark oration "A Time to Break Silence," delivered at New York's Riverside Church in 1967 exactly one year before he was assassinated, King insisted on internationalism over nationalist sentiment. King contended that "such a call for a worldwide fellowship that lifts neighborly concern beyond one's tribe, race, class and nation is in reality a call for an all-embracing and unconditional love for all men."[16] At the end of King's sermon, appropriately titled "The Drum Major Instinct," which dissected the impulse of individuals to be supreme and of nations to rule the world, King declared that "the God I worship has a way of saying, 'Don't play with me. Be still and know that I'm God. And if you don't stop your reckless course, I'll rise up and break the backbone of your power.' And that can happen to America."[17] Martin Luther King Jr.'s role as a dissenter and prophet never diminished his patriotism. True patriots love their country enough to tell it the truth. King never confused a healthy patriotism with a myopic na-

tionalism that often wrapped ethnic bigotry and racial terror in a flag—
and around a cross.

Since September 11, the link between religious belief and terrorist
activity has been emphasized throughout the media and in schoolrooms
and sanctuaries across the nation. But we must remember three crucial
points in thinking of the relationship between religion and terrorism.
First, the political environment in which religious belief springs forth
shapes its social expression. Thus, the fusion of national pride and religious identity—encouraged in certain Muslim states and in our nation
as well—can lead to devastating consequences. Second, it's the extremes
of religious faith about which we should be most concerned. Finally,
terror must be spelled in the plural. In doing so, we underscore how the
oppression that is underwritten by religious belief is experienced as terror by its victims. And we gain as well a better understanding of how
uncritical national pride can fuel the denial of the domestic terror a country may impose on its own citizens.

It cannot be denied that religion pervades the terrorism—and our
response to it—that crumbled the World Trade Center and our national
security. When a Koran was found among the effects left behind in a car
rented by two suspects in the World Trade Center debacle, religious stereotypes immediately flashed. Many in the West believe that Islam encourages fanaticism and a hatred of our way of life. In truth, the Muslim
faith at best preaches peace and human solidarity. As with any religion,
the culture in which it takes root will inevitably influence its expression.

African Christianity, for instance, fused at crucial points with indigenous tribal beliefs to form a powerful and distinct syncretism. In America, the values and experiences of the Pilgrim Fathers shaped their religious understanding of how and where they fit in the world's political order. Hence, many American Christians embraced Manifest Destiny and believed that God backed slavery and the dehumanization of black identity that followed in its wake. Uncritical pride in American identity, leading to American nationalism, fostered vicious beliefs and practices. And in countries where Islamic belief has flourished, including many Arab nations, desperate poverty, coupled with the perception that American imperialism has crippled Middle Eastern stability, has certainly fueled nationalist sentiment and thus fed anti-American attitudes and the embrace of destructive violence by religiously inspired groups.

But the use of violence in the name of religion is not unique to Islam. Christianity and Judaism are rife with examples of adherents claiming God to be the inspiration for their brands of terror. In fact, the most visible expression of any religion, especially to outsiders, is usually its fundamentalist branch. The true believer of any faith willing to kill for religious principles is a blight, whether in Oklahoma or Afghanistan. The terror unleashed in the attacks on the World Trade Center and the Pentagon is not an indictment of belief, but of believers. The twisted, perverted interpretation of religion cannot be allowed to supplant the resourceful spiritual traditions that sustain us. That is why millions of citizens here and around the globe turn immediately to their faith to shield them when terror erupts. When the 9/11 terrorists struck, mosques, temples, synagogues, ashrams, churches, and cathedrals were packed as bishops, imams, rabbis, shamans, priests, and ministers read from holy scriptures and helped believers address the unspeakable depravity they had witnessed. Sometimes, the best defense against the worship of one's country spawned by religious belief is a religiously inspired critique of zealous pride and nationalist sentiment.

The acts of terror on 9/11 remind us of a difficult truth: that religious belief in this nation has often helped to support and impose terror on its victims. The history of slavery brims with theological justifications for continuing the trade in African flesh that began in 1619. The incredible cruelty to black people—viewing them as savages and less than human—found moral support in sermons preached in churches throughout America. More recently, during the civil rights movement, white churches joined forces with white terrorist organizations, including the Ku Klux Klan and White Citizens Council, to impede black progress, even resorting to castration, rape, lynching, and other acts of murder and terror to put down black resistance and rebellion. National pride and white supremacy dovetailed in destructive fashion. Women in our nation have also been subject to forms of terror related to religious belief and practice. Religious bodies have explicitly supported the constant suppression of females rights; for example, the vote, and the control of their reproductive choices. The social and economic inferiority of women has been staked to religious tenets propagated in church sanctuaries as well as in synagogues and mosques. Moreover, extremist views in all religious camps have justified violence toward women, often supported or overlooked by the state, as a legitimate measure of social control.

Finally, the terrors to which lesbians, gays, bisexual, and transgender citizens are vulnerable are often overlooked or scoffed at by most of us who fall outside their ranks. The religious justification for the social stigma of homosexuality—and in some cases, for the violence expressed toward gay and lesbian people—is taken for granted in many quarters of the culture. (In fact, one meaning of pride has been identified with the social and political movement to remove stigma from gay, lesbian, bisexual, and transgender identity, summarized simply in the term "Pride.") To be sure, many will claim that there is hardly a justifiable comparison between what happened on 9/11 and the oppression faced by racial, gender, and sexual minorities. And yet the same bigotry, and the violence it encourages, lay at the base of what we witnessed on 9/11 and the experience of the victims of racism, sexism, and homophobia. At its best, religion provides theological support for the most vulnerable members of our culture and argues against the violence done in God's name to all victims of terror, whether their cause is given global recognition or buried on the back pages of history. In fact, for those who suffer the latter fate, it is even more reason to link their oppression to a suffering we readily understand and acknowledge, and with which we sometimes empathize. In so doing, we meet the nearly universal moral criteria of all religious faiths: to remember victims of all terrors and to seek justice on their behalf, even if the national mood or country's self-image and pride are challenged by our action.

We must also meet the civic criteria of a good society that is politically healthy. A sign of good health is the vigilant effort to protect our civil liberties and the freedoms on which they rest, since, as the truism holds, the first casualty of war is free speech. In the present climate that means, for instance, that we must resist and publicly criticize President Bush's ongoing attempts to broadly expand the use of electronic surveillance to trap terrorists, since it may actually unfairly target American citizens. Moreover, Bush's plan to use secret military tribunals to prosecute terrorists subverts the principle of due process that guarantees democracy. The real terror behind many of the legal maneuvers of the Bush administration at this point is their threat to the moral and legal fabric of the very society he aims to protect. For instance, the Justice Department early on in the "war on terror" announced plans to wiretap conversations between some prisoners and their legal counsel. The problem with such a measure is that the Justice Department can exploit such broad-based powers under the guise of fighting terrorism to otherwise harass and discriminate against certain prisoners. Furthermore, political prisoners in particular are vulnerable to such an agenda. Their critique of American government can be handily punished through discretionary powers exercised by the state. This could turn out to be Orwellian manipulation of the truth at its worst. What's worse is that it would be done in the name of protecting America against a virulent strain of terror when the real harm would be the actions of our own government. The unchecked run of national pride in its basest nationalist mode means trouble for our democracy.

For those who doubt that we could stoop to such manipulation, a refresher course in racial and political history is in order. One need only recall the FBI's COINTELPRO, or Counter Intelligence Program, the government's efforts to put down "black revolutionaries" and others during the 1960s and 1970s. The "crime" of such revolutionaries was that they sought to bridge the gulf between American rhetoric about rights, freedom, and democracy, and the woeful political practices that negated these realities. The government carried out a program of political harassment, invasive technological surveillance, and outright fomenting of political disturbance to flush out ostensible antipatriots. But many of these alleged antipatriots, including figures like Black Panther Bobby Rush, now a highly regarded congressman and ordained minister, were committed to making America a better nation for all its citizens. In fact, in 1969 two American heroes, Fred Hampton and Mark Clark, were assassinated by the Chicago police. The savage murders of Hampton and Clark, members of the Illinois Black Panther Party, remind us how dangerous it is for the government to use unjust methods, including wiretapping, to target political dissidents mislabeled as terrorists.

The racial climate of 1969 seethed with enormous racial tension. Martin Luther King Jr. had been assassinated in 1968, and the civil rights movement was giving way to a more militant brand of black protest. In the wake of King's demise, the black liberation struggle surged, heralding the rise of black power and social revolution. The Black Panther Party for Self-Defense, founded in 1966 by Bobby Seale and Huey Newton in Oakland, California, became the most visible symbol of these changed racial politics.[18] Contrary to public perception, the Black Panther Party was largely concerned with bringing social services to impoverished communities. They started breakfast and educational programs in blighted urban neighborhoods. The Panthers advocated armed self-defense against violent white supremacy. Typical of the biased media coverage that discounted the violence to which the Panthers responded, they were branded as criminals and subversives out to destroy the government. To be sure, some Panthers undeniably engaged in destructive behavior. Just as with bad cops, the actions of a few must not tarnish the achievements of the majority. The Panthers' big goal was to ensure a just society through sustained resistance to political, social, and economic inequality.

Fred Hampton, an extremely charismatic twenty-year-old social activist and organizer, was, in 1969, head of the Illinois branch of the Panthers, which he had joined a year earlier. Hampton had been a gifted student and former NAACP organizer in the Chicago area. Hampton, joined later by seventeen-year-old Mark Clark of the Peoria chapter, led five breakfast programs on the city's West Side, helped to create a free medical clinic, began a door-to-door program to screen for sickle cell anemia, and supported blood drives for Cook County Hospital. Hampton also led the Panthers' efforts to convert and recruit local gangs to assist in class warfare against economic misery. It was Hampton's success that earned him the enmity of his own government, particularly the FBI's Counter Intelligence Program. Armed with dirty tricks and deceitful practices, COINTELPRO undermined revolutionary groups that aimed to bring about true freedom and democracy in America. They amassed a file on Hampton, beginning in 1967, that grew beyond four thousand pages. Further, they planted William O'Neal, a felon who agreed to spy on the Panthers to get his charges dropped, inside the party, where he became Hampton's chief of security.

With help from O'Neal, who drew a diagram of the West Side apartment that served as the Panther headquarters, and under the direction of Cook County State's Attorney Edward V. Hanrahan, more than a dozen police raided the headquarters at 4:30 a.m. on December 4, 1969. Hampton had been drugged by O'Neal with a heavy dose of the depressant secobarbital and could barely wake up when the assault began. Clark was shot pointblank in his chest as he slept with a shotgun in his hands. He reflexively fired the only round discharged by a Panther in the raid. Hampton was in bed with his eight-and-a-half-month pregnant fiancée, Deborah Johnson (now Akua Njeri), when the hail of ninety police shots tore through his bedroom wall. Johnson was injured but survived. Hampton was shot in the shoulder but died when two officers entered his bedroom and shot him pointblank in the head. Several other Panthers were wounded. Not a single policeman served a day in jail for this heinous crime. Hampton and Clark's killings resulted when our government justified its murderous methods with the argument that it was ridding the nation of terrorists. We should remember that now as we combat the plague of terror hatched by figures beyond our nation's borders, and the one that haunts our history from within.

Then, too, we must not forget that even Martin Luther King Jr. was targeted by the FBI for electronic surveillance because he represented a threat to our democracy. King's office, home, and hotels were tapped. FBI head J. Edgar Hoover contended that such surveillance would prove that King was a communist who sought to undermine the American government. King was indeed a radical democrat who sought to force America, as he stated the night before he died, to "Be true to what you said on paper."[19] But this legendary American hero was subject to vicious, antidemocratic procedures in the name of protecting the government. The surveillance of Martin Luther King Jr. only hurt our government in the long run because it failed to concede the legitimacy and political usefulness of dissent. It is chilling to remember that Robert Kennedy, who was then the attorney general, authorized the wiretaps, with the full knowledge of President John F. Kennedy.

If we are to maintain any semblance of fairness, we must bring terrorists before international courts of justice that have proved proficient in prosecuting war criminals from Nuremberg to Bosnia. To do less would be to extend a marred record of American governmental justification of misdeeds in the name of protecting our democracy. The ultimate safeguard against such distortion is to behave justly, even when dealing with the enemies of our country. Otherwise, we are no better than the un-principled and destructive terrorists we condemn.

To be sure, Bush's actions are not the only measures adopted by government officials that should give us pause about the role of the state in enforcing narrow conceptions of the national interest. Some of former Attorney General John Ashcroft's efforts to prevent further terrorism in the wake of September 11 were a frightening example of what Rep. John Conyers of Detroit called Ashcroft's "wartime propaganda machine in full swing."[20] First, in October, 2001, Ashcroft commanded U.S. attorneys throughout the nation to track down and "voluntarily" interview nearly five thousand men between the ages of eighteen and thirty-three who came to the United States after January 2000 on nonimmigrant visas, mostly from Muslim countries. Next, Muslims around the country were secretively detained after 9/11. Then, in March 2002, Ashcroft expanded the campaign of racial profiling by targeting another three thousand Middle Eastern men between the ages of eighteen and forty-six who came to this country between October 2001 and February 2002.

Finally, the federal government in March 2002 conducted a series of raids on homes, businesses, and charities in Northern Virginia deemed to have financial links to terrorist groups like al-Qaida and Hamas. In isolation, these events signal a scary assault on the civil liberties and personal dignity of fellow human beings. In tandem, they represent the vicious persecution of an ethnic group not unlike that endured by suspected supporters of Japan during World War II. Ashcroft made two specious arguments at the time to support the Justice Department's actions. First, he argued that racial profiling of Muslim men yielded significant leads. Second, he said that interviews of Muslim men have created better relations between law enforcement and Arab Americans.

As for the high yield of leads, unidentified law enforcement officials asserted that little useful intelligence resulted from such efforts. The government's shoddy system of tracking immigrants and visas led the author of a Justice Department report to conclude that officials were able to interview only 2,261 men from the list of 4,793 Muslim men originally targeted. (It is easy to imagine critics saying, "There weren't nearly 5,000 men profiled, but only 2,261." But that is 2,261 too many without adequate cause beyond their ethnic and national affiliations). The report admits that of this number, only three were arrested on criminal charges and none was charged with terrorism.

The argument that racial profiling of Muslim men enhances relations between law enforcement and Arab Americans would be laughable if it weren't tragically ill informed. (By that logic, law enforcement could better its relations with white men by profiling males between twenty-five and sixty-five suspected of cheating on their tax returns or accused of battering their wives.) To cite another example that proves the flawed logic of such an approach, the efforts of the Justice Department to foster better relations between law enforcement and black men—which has led to skyrocketing incarceration rates for mostly minor infractions—is a massive failure from most black people's point of view.

The use of racial profiling, indefensible detentions, and unjust raids only perpetuates the belief that our nation is practicing reverse terrorism. If we are to root out terrorism, we must make certain that our efforts don't negate the very principles to which we claim allegiance: justice, truth, and freedom. If we deploy unjust practices to attain just ends, we not only leave a legally twisted trail of justifications, but we undercut the ethical legs upon which we stand in the resistance to terrorism. The lamentable justifications for our highly questionable practices resemble the arguments made, if more crudely, against people of Japanese descent during World War II who turned out to be model citizens, especially after they were released from internment camps and enjoyed the freedoms for which many of them had eagerly fought.

Bush's actions—and Ashcroft's pattern of response when he was attorney general—signify a new strain of nationalist sentiment and uncritical national pride that has swept America: patriotic correctness. Patriotic correctness is a variety of PC that, interestingly enough, is largely propagated by the very forces who decry old-style PC: political correctness. Black Americans have been discouraged from patriotic correctness because of our tortured relationship to a country that has exploited our unpaid labor in slavery, our cultural genius in servitude and freedom, and our sacrificial service in the armed forces. Frederick Douglass piercingly summed up the black view of patriotism in the nineteenth century, and for many blacks even today, when he probed the meaning of Independence Day in a legendary speech:

What to the American slave is your Fourth of July? I answer a day that reveals to him, more than all other days of the year, the gross injustice and cruelty to which he is the constant victim. To him your celebration is a sham; your boasted liberty an unholy license; your national greatness, swelling vanity; your sounds of rejoicing are empty and heartless; your denunciations of tyrants, brass-fronted impudence; your shouts of liberty and equality, hollow mockery; your prayers and hymns, your sermons and thanksgivings, with all your religious parade and solemnity, are to him mere bombast, fraud, deception, impiety, and hypocrisy—a thin veil to cover up crimes which would disgrace a nation of savages. There is not a nation on the earth guilty of practices more shocking and bloody than are the people of these United States at this very hour.

Go where you may, search where you will, roam through all the monarchies and despotisms of the Old World, travel through South America, search out every abuse and when you have found the last, lay your facts by the side of the every-day practices of this nation, and you will say with me that, for revolting barbarity and shameless hypocrisy, America reigns without a rival.[21]

Each year as the country celebrates its birthday on July 4, black Americans reflect on our place in a nation that we have loved enough to criticize. The torn emotions most blacks feel are captured in an engaging and utterly honest book whose title says it all, *Yet a Stranger: Why Black Americans Still Don't Feel At Home.*[22] Authored by syndicated columnist and social critic Deborah Mathis, *Yet a Stranger* probes the ambivalence blacks feel in being loyal but tortured citizens of a nation whose promise is bigger than its practice. The first words of Mathis's opening chapter, titled "Which Way to the Promised Land?" capture the reason for black ambivalence: The nation can't make up its mind whether it loves or loathes us. "I love the old girl despite her nasty ways. I know she needs me. I think she knows it too. Still, she can be so difficult at times. So ornery and ungrateful. Cruel on occasion. Wicked. Inflicting pain and tribulation just for the heck of it, it seems. Yet every time, just as I am about to collapse under her tiresome demands or explode with rage from her abuse, she pulls me to her bosom and rocks me with promises. One moment I am her curse, the next her beloved."

Mathis neatly sums up a view of America from its darker side that many whites have never confronted. During July 4 celebrations, many blacks spurn the holiday altogether, because the freedom celebrated is segregated by skin color and even class at times. They resonate with Langston Hughes's plaintive poem, "Let America Be America Again," when he says, "America never was America to me /. . . (There's never been equality for me, / Nor freedom in this 'homeland of the free.')." Other blacks are torn. On the one hand, they completely resonate with their bitterly disappointed brothers and sisters. On the other hand, they acknowledge that black blood, sweat, and tears have built this country. Hence, they echo Martin Luther King Jr. when he declared, "I ain't goin' nowhere." King was responding, perhaps, to mean-spirited critics who would dare deny blacks who fought for the nation's freedom their right to criticize America in love and as a gesture of profound patriotism. Such critics use a pat line that is truly trite: "If you don't like America, go back to where you came from." But as Mathis says of blacks, "Most of us—91 percent—were born and have lived only here."

In the aftermath of 9/11, our jangled nerves are no excuse to demand silence or suppression of honest disagreement over the nation's meaning as a sign of loyalty. It is even more a reason to embrace the freedom of expression that pushed the forefathers to leave tyranny and embrace democracy. Mathis's book reminds us of this fact. It is a critical engagement with the social, political, economic, and racial forces that conspire to keep the nation bitterly divided and radically unjust. Mathis insightfully examines the racial landscape—including unconscious white racism, prejudice in the classroom, inequality in financial institutions, the racially charged rhetoric of self-help, promotion of Eurocentric values, crime and unequal punishment, affirmative action, and the like. These factors pit majority culture, with its often unexamined assumptions, against minority culture, with its often unheeded arguments.

It is noteworthy that Mathis is critical but not hopeless about America. "Of course I realize her neurosis is dangerous and that I should probably run off. That would show her. But I am a sucker for the good in her, which is a good too good to leave. So here I stay, battered but bewitched. What can I say? She is my country, my home." But Mathis is a hardheaded, clear-eyed realist when it comes to race and country. "Yet black Americans, descendants of the stolen Africans, still do not have equal footing with white Americans who share with us a nation. This is our home, but we do not enjoy its full range of comforts." Chris Rock acidly captured the conflicted black feeling toward America when he said, "If you're black, America's like the uncle that paid your way through college—but molested you."[23]

The most vocal advocates of patriotic correctness have rarely confronted the compelling reasons behind the persistent ambivalence most blacks feel when loyalty to the nation is being discussed. I got a strong whiff of the new PC—and the brutal racial contradictions that rest at the heart of national pride—at two sporting events I witnessed: the Super Bowl XXXVI in New Orleans, in January 2002, and later that year, in February, the NBA All-Star game in Philadelphia.

I attended the Super Bowl in New Orleans with an American hero, a black man who happens to be a fireman, a powerful symbol of national pride in the aftermath of September 11. With all the patriotic flare that engulfed the sporting world's most ballyhooed game, I got a glimpse through him of the hidden treasure of character that often goes unrecognized in our nation. Stanley Perkins is a captain in the Los Angeles Fire Department, one of about thirty blacks to achieve that honor on a force of more than four thousand firefighters. Until Perkins achieved his rank in 1993, the fifty-eight-year-old fireman had been an engineer for fifteen years, driving the engine and pumping the water to his firefighting colleagues. For the first nine years of his career, Perkins risked his life by fighting fires in buildings, on prairies, on city streets, and in the valleys that dot the California landscape.

But the heat he confronted in Los Angeles paled in comparison to the fires of poverty and bigotry Perkins encountered growing up in Louisiana and California. Perkins was reared in Amite, Louisiana, a rural outpost from New Orleans, where he would visit his relatives on occasion, a big outing for a young black boy of modest means from the country. When he was twelve, Perkins moved with his mother and several siblings to Compton, California, a city that would be immortalized a generation later for its gang violence in the lyrics of West Coast rap group N.W.A. Perkins and his family eventually relocated to the projects in the infamous Watts ghetto of Los Angeles. Perkins witnessed the Watts riot of 1965, seeing firsthand what Martin Luther King Jr. meant when he said after touring Watts that "a riot is 'the language of the unheard.'" After surviving what King termed a "holocaust" in Watts, Perkins in 1969 joined the fire department as one of its first few blacks. [24]

Although Perkins cherishes his career of public service, he has on occasion faced racism from within the ranks of the fire department. For instance, several years ago he was nearly killed, sideswiped by a white crew from a competing station as they refused to slow down at his request while approaching his truck. It was later apparent that their obnoxious behavior was driven by race. But Perkins persisted, overcoming professional and personal obstacles to achieve status and distinction in the department. Contrary to the perceptions of disgruntled critics of affirmative action, black firemen often work twice as hard to secure their success, a view that Perkins's career amply supports. As I sat with Perkins at the Super Bowl, taking in the hyperpatriotism that bathed the game's proceedings, he showed his pride as a fireman in joining with others to salute the achievements of his colleagues in New York during the September 11 attacks on the World Trade Center. But he lamented the near total media eclipse of the courage of the twelve black firemen who lost their lives that day.

We discussed the brouhaha sparked by the decision to mark the recovery and replanting of the American flag at the World Trade Center site by white firemen through a statue of the occasion. We also discussed the lamentable decision to scrap the statue once it was determined that the bravery of black and Latino firefighters should be acknowledged by casting the trio in multicultural face. Critics who were enthralled with one PC—patriotic correctness—charged their adversaries with the old PC—political correctness. But defenders of the move to acknowledge the multiple races and ethnicities that perished together that day viewed it as a matter of justice.

In New Orleans, I thought of Perkins's quiet heroism as I witnessed the pageantry of patriotism at the Super Bowl: a pregame video tape of football players reading the Declaration of Independence; a video of former presidents Ford, Carter, Bush, and Clinton joining Nancy Reagan (standing in for her husband, former president Reagan, whose voice was also heard) in quoting Abraham Lincoln; Paul McCartney singing his

9/11-themed song "Freedom"; and Patti LaBelle, Wynona, Yolanda Adams, and James Ingram joining Barry Manilow to sing "Let Freedom Ring," penned by Manilow in 2000 to commemorate the two hundredth anniversary of the U.S. Constitution. The Founding Fathers were thus well represented at Super Bowl XXXVI. At best, they were ambiguous about racial justice and democracy. At worst, they were outright hypocrites. Still, their valor and vision were amply cited at this magnificent sporting event. As I thought of the Founding Fathers' mixed record of monumental heroism and moral hypocrisy, I concluded that anyone who says that giving black heroes their just due is a morally flawed gesture, a mere nod to reverse racism, is sadly misinformed. Such Americans are most deserving of honor, and Captain Stanley Perkins is their perfect symbol.

As was true for Super Bowl XXXVI, and the 2002 Winter Olympics in Salt Lake City, the 2002 NBA All-Star game was awash in political sentiment that is usually scorned, or at least avoided, at sporting events. When track stars Tommy Smith and John Carlos raised their gloved black fists at the 1968 Olympics in solidarity with the struggle for justice back home, they had their medals snatched, and their credibility and careers ruined. And when Muhammad Ali in the late 1960s forfeited his World Heavyweight Boxing championship in opposition to the war in Vietnam, he was roundly condemned. The American public today celebrates his mere presence, as they did at the 2002 NBA All-Star game, now that he is mostly mute and largely unthreatening.

America makes no pretense of being opposed to the new PC. American sports—and how far behind can Hollywood be?—are now dedicated to the cause of hammering home the message: America is not only right but uniquely blessed by God. In the past, that kind of thinking got us into deep trouble. After all, we said the same thing when we defended slavery, turned away a ship of Jews who sought entry into the nation after fleeing the Holocaust, and interred American citizens of Japanese descent in makeshift concentration camps during World War II. Now that America is nearly drunk on public and political displays of American loyalty—the most visible signs of an exorbitant national pride—we ought to be careful about thinking that we can't be wrong.

In fact, a healthy dose of skepticism about patriotic correctness was injected into "America the Beautiful" at the All-Star game by singers Angie Stone and Alicia Keys. On the one hand, they implied their dissent. On the other hand, they stated it outright. While singing the words of the song that many think should be our nation's anthem, Stone and Keys seamlessly segued into a thoughtful, soulful rendition of portions of "Lift Every Voice," the black national anthem. In so doing, they were not only tastefully alluding to their cultural heritage but insisting that the entire truth of the American struggle for democracy be celebrated. Moreover, when the singers suggested that God bless America— *"and everyone"*—they were making as resistive a political gesture as one might make now in such settings. It was refreshing to witness the conscience and courage of touted young artists who took the lead in redefining national pride in a way that enhances the nation's civic health.

It can be argued that Stone and Keys's gesture was a glancing tribute to the "radical revolution of values" envisioned by Martin Luther King Jr.[25] King's vision grew from "the privilege and the burden of all of us who deem ourselves bound by allegiances and loyalties which are broader and deeper than nationalism and which go beyond our nation's self-defined goals and positions."[26] King argued that a "true revolution of values will soon cause us to question the fairness and justice of our past and present policies."[27] King summarized his views in a poignant passage that is a prophetic warning against the vice of narrow national self-interest and the sin of unquestioning national pride:

> A true revolution of values will soon look uneasily on the glaring contrast of poverty and wealth. With righteous indignation, it will look across the seas and see individual capitalists of the West investing huge sums of money in Asia, Africa and South America, only to take the profits out with no concern for the social betterment of the countries, and say: "This is not just." It will look at our alliance with the landed gentry of Latin America and say: "This is not just." The Western arrogance of feeling that it has everything to teach others and nothing to learn from them is not just. A true revolution of values will lay hands on the world order and say of war: "This way of settling differences is not just." A nation that continues year after year to spend more on military

defense than on programs of social uplift is approaching spiritual death. America, the richest and most powerful nation in the world, can well lead the way in this revolution of values. There is nothing, except a tragic death wish, to prevent us from reordering our priorities, so that the pursuit of peace will take precedence over the pursuit of war. . . . A genuine revolution of values means in the final analysis that our loyalties must become ecumenical rather than sectional. Every nation must now develop an overriding loyalty to mankind as a whole in order to preserve the best in their individual societies."[28]

Notes

INTRODUCTION

1. Lawrence C. Becker, "Pride," vol. 3 (P–W) of *Encyclopedia of Ethics,*
   2nd ed., ed. Lawrence C. Becker and Charlotte B. Becker (New York:
   Routledge, 2001), 1375.

2. Craig Brown, "Out With the Old Deadly Sins, In With the New,"
   Scotsman (Edinburgh), February 7, 2005.

3. Ibid.

4. Ibid.

5. Ibid.

6. 1 John 4:20–21 (King James Version).

7. Amy Diluna, Joe Dziemianowicz, and Michelle Megna, "Sin Is In:
   Chances to behave badly abound this summer. Here're where to look
   for them," *Daily News* (New York), June 10, 2004.

8. Ibid.

9. Ibid.

10. Philip Chard, "It's a sin we can't behave better," *Milwaukee Journal
    Sentinel*, August 3, 2004.

11. Ibid.

12. I follow here philosopher Michele M. Moody-Adams's distinction be-
    tween self-respect and self-esteem. The two, she argues, are confused by
    philosopher John Rawls. As Adams argues: "Rawls contends that 'a
    person's sense of his own value' is equivalent to that person's 'secure
    conviction that his conception of his good, his plan of life, is worth

carrying out.' Rawls also claims that 'self-respect implies a confidence in one's ability, so far as it is within one's power, to fulfill one's intentions. Like other critics of this claim, I think that what Rawls describes here is not self-respect but the phenomenon of self-esteem. Moreover, the distinction between self-esteem and self-respect is crucial. How else can we understand that a person might lose confidence in the worth of some particular life plan without at the same time questioning her value as a person? People can sometimes refine, revise, or relinquish a life plan (or some portion of it) should circumstances require them to do so. This is because self-respect is both more fundamental, and less fragile, than self-esteem.

"But while self-esteem—confidence in one's life plan—is distinct from self-respect—a due sense of one's own worth—severe diminutions in self-esteem may nonetheless have devastating effects on self-respect." See Michele M. Moody-Adams, "Race, Class, and the Social Construction of Self-Respect," *The Philosophical Forum*, vol. 24, no. 1–3, Fall–Spring 1992–93, 254.

CHAPTER ONE

1. Stanford M. Lyman, *The Seven Deadly Sins: Society and Evil,* rev. ed. (Dix Hills, NY: General Hall, Inc., 1989), 136.

2. Ibid.

3. Ibid.; Matthew Baasten, *Pride According to Gregory the Great: A Study of the Moralia* (Lewiston, NY: Edwin Mellen Press), 77–78; Kim Campbell, "Is sin in?" *Christian Science Monitor*, August 7, 2003, 15; Joseph J. Spengler, "Social Science and the Collectivization of Hubris," *Political Science Quarterly*, vol. 87, no. 1 (March., 1972): 3.

4. Cited in Baasten, 78.

5. Ibid., 79.

6. Cited in Lyman, 136.

7. For a brilliant biography of Augustine, see James J. O'Donnell, *Augustine: A New Biography* (New York: Ecco, 2005).

8. Lyman, 163.

9. Cited in Lyman, 163.

10. Augustine, *City of God*, 12.13, 14.13, cited in Reinhold Niebuhr, *The Nature and Destiny of Man,* vol. 1, *Human Nature* (1941; repr., Louisville: Westminster/John Knox Press, 1996), 186–87.

11. Cited in Lyman, 164.

12. Ibid.

13. Ibid.

14. Baasten, 119–38; Eileen Sweeney, "Vice and Sin (Ia IIae, qq. 71–89), in *The Ethics of Aquinas,* ed. Stephen J. Pope (Washington, DC: Georgetown University Press, 2002), 159; Jean Porter, *The Recovery of Virtue: The Relevance of Aquinas for Christian Ethics* (Louisville: Westminster/John Knox Press, 1990), 110. Of course, as Alasdair MacIntyre argues, Aquinas attempts to overcome the conflict in traditions of moral reflection on justice between Augustine and Aristotle— to boot, for Augustine, the sin of the Romans, who inherited Greek ideas of virtue, was their pride, manifest in their hunger for glory, against which Augustine places the Christian value of humility, while, MacIntyre notes, pride as a vice is absent in Aristotle. Sweeney, 167, n33, and Alasdair MacIntyre, *Whose Justice? Which Rationality?* (Notre Dame, IN: University of Notre Dame Press, 1988), 155, 163.

15. Stephen J. Pope, "Overview of the Ethics of Thomas Aquinas," in *The Ethics of Aquinas* (see note 14), 45; Sweeney, 163.

16. Ibid., 45–46.

17. Sweeney, 162–63.

18. Cited in Pope, 45.

19. Cited in Sweeney, 163.

20. See Sweeney, especially 152–54, 163.

21. Ibid., 152.

22. Spengler, 2. Also, variants of hubris, including hubrizein, hubristes, and hubrisma showed up in fourth and fifth century Athenian prose authors. See David Cohen, "Sexuality, Violence, and the Athenian Law of 'Hubris'" *Greece & Rome*, 2nd ser., vol. 38, no. 2 (Oct. 1991): 172.

23. See Joseph Pieper, *The Four Cardinal Virtues* (Notre Dame, IN: University of Notre Dame Press, 1966).

24. C. M. Bowra, *The Greek Experience* (New York: New American Library, 1959), 99–101; Walter Raymond Agard, *The Greek Mind* (New York, 1959), 68, both cited in Spengler, 3.

25. Aristotle, *The Nicomachean Ethics,* trans. with an introduction by David Ross; rev. by J. L. Ackrill and J. O. Urmson (1925; repr., New York: Oxford University Press, 1980), 91.

26. Alasdair MacIntyre, *A Short History of Ethics: A History of Moral Philosophy from the Homeric Age to the Twentieth Century* (1966; repr., London: Routledge, 1998), 79. This is not to argue that Aristotle didn't at all challenge social difference; he didn't do so based on contemporary claims to social equality but because the wealthy often made claims to respect on a faulty basis. He believed in an aristocracy that was truly morally superior, not one that made its claim to superiority based on power or money. "In ancient Greek society there were large differences of social status. Men who were descended from superior families or enjoyed supe-

rior wealth respected themselves on that account, and expected others to show respect. Aristotle opposed this social differentiation, not because of the modern dogma that all human beings deserve equal respect, but because men based their claims to respect on the wrong grounds, on what came to them by fortune, not on their own moral qualities." D. S. Huthinson, "Ethics," in *The Cambridge Companion to Aristotle,* ed. Jonathan Barnes (Cambridge: Cambridge University Press, 1995), 226.

27. Aristotle, *The Nicomachean Ethics* [Ross and others], 89. For "great-souled person," see Aristotle, *The Nicomachean Ethics* [trans. with historical introduction by Christopher Rowe, philosophical introduction and commentary by Sarah Broadie], (New York: Oxford University Press, 2002), 148. For "magnanimous man" see Aristotle, *The Nicomachean Ethics,* trans. J. A. K. Thomson, rev. with notes and appendices by Hugh Tredennick, introduction and further reading by Jonathan Barnes (1953; repr., New York: Penguin Books, 2004), 94.

28. Aristotle [Ross and others], 89.

29. Ibid.

30. Ibid., 90; Aristotle [Rowe and Broadie], 148.

31. Hutchinson, 227.

32. Aristotle [Ross and others], 90; Aristotle [Rowe and Broadie], 148.

33. Aristotle [Ross and others], 95.

34. Ibid., 41.

35. Ibid., 90.

36. Ibid., 91.

37. MacIntyre, *A Short History of Ethics*, 78.

38. Alexander Pope, *An Essay on Man,* Epistle 1, 4, line 123; Jonathan Swift, *Gulliver's Travels,* cited in Lucius W. Elder, "The Pride of the Yahoo,"

Modern Language Notes, vol. 35, no. 4 (April 1920): 206; David Hume, *Treatise of Human Nature,* bk. 3, sec. 2, 595, 596, 601, cited in Elder, 207; Spinoza, *Ethics*, 4, prop. 56, cited in Elder, 211.

39. Elder, "The Pride of the Yahoo," 206.

40. William K. Frankena, *Ethics*, 2nd ed. (Englewood Cliffs: Prentice-Hall, Inc., 1973), 62.

41. Alisdair MacIntyre, *After Virtue: A Study in Moral Theory* (Notre Dame, IN: Notre Dame Press, 1981).

42. Stanley Hauerwas, *Character and the Christian Life: A Study in Theological Ethics* (San Antonio: Trinity University Press, 1975); *Vision and Virtue: Essays in Christian Theological Reflection* (Notre Dame, IN: University of Notre Dame Press, 1981); *A Community of Character: Toward a Constructive Christian Social Ethic*; and *The Peaceable Kingdom* (Notre Dame, IN: University of Notre Dame Press, 1983).

43. Proverbs 16:18 (King James Version).

44. Psalms 8:4 (King James Version).

45. Job 38:4 (Revised Standard Version).

46. James Melvin Washington, "The Difficulty of Going Home: Reflections on Race and Modernity," *Christian Century*, vol. 101, no. 25 (Aug. 15–22): 777.

47. Arthur Lovejoy, "Pride in Eighteenth-Century Thought," *Modern Language Notes*, vol. 36, no. 1 (Jan. 1921): 35.

48. *King James Version*, Mark 12:30–31.

CHAPTER TWO

1. Ralph Ellison, *Invisible Man,* 2nd ed. (1952; repr., New York: Vintage International, 1995).

2. Ralph Ellison, *Shadow and Act* (1964; repr., New York: Vintage International, 1995).

3. Toni Morrison, *Song of Solomon* (New York: Random House, 1977).

4. For the best collection of his essays, see James Baldwin, *The Price of the Ticket: Collected Nonfiction 1948–1985* (New York: St. Martin's/Marek, 1985).

5. James Baldwin, *Go Tell It on the Mountain* (New York: Modern Library, 1995 [1953]), and *Notes of a Native Son* (1955; repr., Boston: Beacon Press, 1984).

6. Lerone Bennett, *What Manner of Man: A Biography of Martin Luther King, Jr.* (Chicago: Johnson Publishing Co., 1968).

CHAPTER THREE

1. Chris Rock, in his 1999 HBO comedy special, *Bigger & Blacker*, quoted in Jesse Berrett, "A Piece of the Rock," *City Pages* (Minneapolis/St. Paul), vol. 20, no. 973.

2. Noel Ignatiev, *How the Irish Became White* (New York: Routledge Press, 1995), and Karen Brodkin, *How the Jews Became White Folks & What That Says About Race in America* (New Brunswick: Rutgers University Press, 1998).

3. The logic of blacks not being fully human was reflected in the theology and social thought of American culture during slavery and afterward, sentiments that were codified in the 1857 Supreme Court decision in Scott v. Sanford (the Dred Scott case), where Chief Justice Roger B. Taney concluded that blacks were only three-fifths human and had "no rights a white man is bound to respect."

4. There is a growing literature on the socially constructed meanings of whiteness. For some of the best of this literature, see David Roediger,

The Wages of Whiteness: Race and the Making of the American Working Class (New York: Verso, 1991); David Roediger, *Towards the Abolition of Whiteness: Essays on Race, Politics, and Working Class History* (New York: Verso, 1994); Theodore W Allen, *The Invention of the White Race: Volume One: Racial Oppression and Social Control* (New York: Verso, 1994); Fred Pfeil, *White Guys: Studies in Postmodern Domination and Difference* (New York: Verso, 1995); Jessie Daniels, *White Lies: Race, Class, Gender, and Sexuality in White Supremacist Discourse* (New York: Routledge, 1997); Matt Wray and Annalee Newitz, eds., *White Trash: Race and Class in America* (New York: Routledge, 1997); Michelle Fine, Lois Weis, Linda C. Powell, and L. Mun Wong, eds., *Off White: Readings on Race, Power, and Society* (New York: Routledge, 1997).

5. Arthur Schlesinger Jr., *The Disuniting of America* (Knoxville, TN: Whittle Direct Books, 1991).

6. Renato Rosaldo, *Culture & Truth: The Remaking of Social Analysis* (Boston: Beacon Press, 1983, 1993), 68–87.

7. For a small sample of such criticism, see: Todd Gitlin, *The Twilight of Common Dreams: Why America is Wracked by Culture Wars* (New York: Metropolitan Books, 1995); Michael Tomasky, *Left For Dead: The Life, Death and Possible Resurrection of Progressive Politics in America* (New York: Free Press, 1996); Arthur Schlesinger Jr., *The Disuniting of America* (Knoxville, TN: Whittle Direct Books, 1991); and Richard Bernstein, *The Dictatorship of Virtue: Multiculturalism and the Battle for America's Future* (New York: Knopf, 1994).

8. See Michael Eric Dyson, *Reflecting Black: African-American Cultural Criticism* (Minneapolis: University of Minnesota Press, 1993); *Making Malcolm: The Myth and Meaning of Malcolm X* (New York: Oxford

University Press, 1994); *Between God and Gangsta Rap: Bearing Witness to Black Culture* (New York: Oxford University Press, 1996); and *Race Rules: Navigating the Color Line* (New York: Addison-Wesley, 1996).

9. Tomasky, *Left For Dead*, 10, 15, 16, 17.

10. In all fairness, the students pirated this notion from an article written by scholar Adolph Reed castigating several black public intellectuals. In his essay, Reed implied that I was a minstrel because of my occasional quotation of rap lyrics in public lectures. See Adolph Reed, *Class Notes: Posing As Politics and Other Thoughts on the American Scene* (New York: New Press, 2000), 77–90.

CHAPTER FOUR

1. For an interesting, but flawed, scholarly examination of black pride— and negative dimensions of black culture, for instance, the expression of prejudice toward other groups, especially Jews—which concludes that black pride does not lead to intolerance for other groups, or a rejection of common American values, see Paul M. Sniderman and Thomas Piazza, *Black Pride and Black Prejudice* (Princeton: Princeton University Press, 2002).

2. Lawrence Otis Graham, *Our Kind of People: Inside America's Black Upper Class* (New York: HarperCollins Publishers, 1999); Michael Eric Dyson, *Is Bill Cosby Right? Or Has the Black Middle Class Lost Its Mind?* (New York: Basic Civitas Books, 2005).

3. Lawrence Otis Graham, *Member of the Club: Reflections on Life in a Racially Polarized World* (New York: HarperCollins, 1995).

4. Kweisi Mfume, with Ron Stodghill II, *No Free Ride: From the Mean Streets to the Mainstream* (New York: One World/Ballantine, 1997).

1. Gloria Ladson-Billings, "It's Your World, I'm Just Trying to Explain It: Understanding Our Epistemological and Methodological Challenges," in *9/11 In American Culture*, ed. Norman K. Denzin and Yvonna S. Lincoln (New York: Altamira Press, 2003), 254.

2. Ibid., 255.

3. Ibid.

4. Ibid.

5. Martha Nussbaum, *For Love of Country?* (Boston: Beacon Press, 2002), x.

6. Reinhold Niebuhr, "The Atomic Bomb," *Christianity and Society* 10 (Fall 1945), cited in *Niebuhr and His Age: Reinhold Niebuhr's Prophetic Role and Legacy* by Charles C. Brown, new ed. (Harrisburg, PA: Trinity Press International, 2002), 123.

7. Reinhold Niebuhr, "The MacArthur Episode," *Christianity and Society* 16 (Summer 1951): 3, cited in Brown, *Niebuhr and His Age*, 150–51.

8. Martin Luther King Jr., "The Drum Major Instinct," in *A Testament of Hope: The Essential Writings and Speeches of Martin Luther King, Jr.,* ed. James Melvin Washington (1986; repr., San Francisco: Harper San Francisco, 1991), 265.

9. Rui J.P. de Figueiredo Jr., and Zachary Elkins, "Are Patriots Bigots? An Inquiry into the Vices of In-Group Pride," *American Journal of Political Science*, vol. 47, no. 1 (Jan. 2003): 178.

10. Ibid.

11. Ibid.

12. Martin Luther King Jr., "The American Dream," in Washington, *A Testament of Hope,* 208.

13. Martin Luther King Jr., "I Have a Dream," in Washington, *A Testament of Hope,* 219.

14. King, "The American Dream," 208.

15. King, "The Drum Major Instinct," 265.

16. Martin Luther King Jr., "A Time to Break Silence," in Washington, *A Testament of Hope,* 242.

17. King, "The Drum Major Instinct," 265.

18. For a sample of the literature on the Black Panther Party, see Philip Foner, ed., *The Black Panthers Speak,* 2nd ed. (1970; repr., Cambridge, MA: Da Capo Press, 2002); Ruth-Marion Baruch and Pirkle Jones, *Black Panthers 1968* (Los Angeles: Greybull Press, 2002); Bobby Seale, *Seize the Time: The Story of the Black Panther Party and Huey P. Newton* (1970; repr., Baltimore: Black Classic Press, 1997); David Hilliard and Donald Weise, eds., *The Huey Newton Reader* (New York: Seven Stories Press, 2002); Kathleen Cleaver and George Katsiaficas, eds., *Liberation, Imagination, and the Black Panther Party: A New Look at the Panthers and Their Legacy* (New York: Routledge, 2001); Charles Jones, ed., *The Black Panther Party Reconsidered* (Baltimore: Black Classic Press, 1998); Elaine Brown, *A Taste of Power: A Black Woman's Story* (New York: Pantheon Books, 1992); and David Hilliard and Lewis Cole, *This Side of Glory: The Autobiography of David Hilliard and the Story of the Black Panther Party* (1993; repr., Chicago: Lawrence Hill Books, 2001).

19. Martin Luther King Jr. "I See the Promised Land," in Washington, *A Testament of Hope,* 282.

20. Congressman John Conyers Jr., Press Release (#107–153#), "Conyers Calls Ashcroft Report Wartime Propaganda," March 20, 2002.

21. Frederick Douglass, "What To The Slave Is The Fourth Of July?" in *Masterpieces of Negro Eloquence: The Best Speeches Delivered by the Negro From the Days of Slavery to the Present Time,* ed. Alice Moore Dunbar (1914; repr., New York: G.K. Hall & Co., 1997), 47–48.

22. Deborah Mathis, *Yet a Stranger: Why Black Americans Still Don't Feel At Home* (New York: Warner Books, 2002).

23. Cited in Sam Delaney, "Pushing the Envelope," *Guardian* (Manchester, UK), Saturday, Feb. 26, 2005.

24. Martin Luther King Jr., "Next Stop: The North," in Washington, *A Testament of Hope,* 192.

25. King, "A Time to Break Silence," 240.

26. Ibid., 234.

27. Ibid., 240.

28. Ibid., 241, 242.

Index

September 11, 2001 (9/11), 88–
        93, 97, 106; patriotic
        correctness and, 111, 112,
        114
Seven Deadly Sins, 2
sexism, 100
Shadow and Act (Eliot), 31
Shakur, Tupac, 55
shame, 77
signifying, 33–35, 79
sin, 2–5, 9–14, 87, 117; vice and,
        20, 22, 24, 26. *See also*
        morality; religion; vice;
        virtue
skepticism, 22, 116
skin-color, 62–65, 67. *See also*
        beauty; race
slavery, 98–99, 108–109, 116,
        125n.3. *See also* blacks; race
Smith, Stephen, 54
Smith, Tommy, 115
Snipes, Wesley, 64
social criticism, 37–42
social differences, 122–23n.26.
        See also class
social justice. *See* justice
social organizations, 71, 74. *See
        also* elitism; Jack and Jill;
        Links
social systems, 95
society, 30
solidarity, 50, 52, 67, 97, 115
Solzhenitsyn, Alexander, 30
Song of Solomon (Morrison), 34
sorority, 78
soul, 11, 15–16, 26
South America, 117
Spinoza, Benedict de, 17

spiritual death, 117
standardized tests, 70
Stanford University, 69
stereotypes, 97
Stone, Angie, 116–18
stories, 25. *See also* narratives;
        writing
superbia (hubris), 10
Super Bowl XXXVI (2002), 112,
        114–15
superiority, 55
supremacy, 61. *See also* hate
        organizations; specific
        supremacist groups; whites
Supreme Court, U.S., 125n.3
Sweeney, Eileen, 12
Swift, Jonathan, 17
symbolism, race and, 69
syncretism, 98

Taney, Roger B., 125n.3
temperance, 14, 16
Tennyson, Alfred, 41
terrorism: America and, 88–92;
        blacks and, 102–105;
        democracy and, 101–102;
        dissent and, 93–96; racial
        profiling and, 106–108;
        religion and, 97–100. *See
        also* September 11; violence
"Testament of Reuben," 10
Testament of the Twelve Prophets,
        10
"The Drum Major Instinct"
        (King), 96
theology, 20
Thomas, Clarence, 65
Thoreau, Henry David, 39, 84

Till, Emmett, 88
Tomasky, Michael, 51–53
Tony Soprano (TV character), 4
transformation, 82
transgender, 100
tribalism, 52
truth, 4, 108
Twin Towers, 90. *See also*
    September 11; World Trade
    Center

Union, Gabrielle, 64
United States, 109; culture in, 4;
    Department of Education,
    66, 70–71; Supreme Court,
    125n.3. *See also* civil
    liberties; democracy;
    dissent; nationalism; *under*
    patriotic
universality, 51–54
universal moral criteria, 100. *See
    also* morality; religion
University of Pennsylvania, 55

vainglory, 9, 10, 93. *See also* glory
values, 95, 111, 117, 118
vanity, 4, 6, 7, 16, 24, 26, 109
vernacular, 19, 35. *See also*
    signifying; voice
vice, 12, 14, 45, 87, 117; sin and,
    20, 22, 24, 26; virtue and,
    2–5, 9, 15, 17, 121n.14.
    See also morality;
    philosophy; religion; sin;
    virtue
Vietnam War, 94, 96, 115
violence, 99–100. *See also*
    terrorism

Virginia, 106
virtue, 1–5, 9, 26, 45, 121n.14;
    Aristotle and, 15, 17–19;
    nationalism and, 85. *See
    also* morality; philosophy;
    religion; sin; vice
visas, 107
Vision and Virtue (Hauerwas), 19
voice, 54, 56, 79. *See also* Ellison;
    Keys; hip-hop; writing
vouchers, 70. *See also* education

Walden Pond, 39. *See also*
    Thoreau
war, 94, 101, 104, 117, 118;
    propaganda and, 106
Washington, Denzel, 64, 77, 79
Washington, James, 23
Watts, J. C., 68
Watts riots (1965), 113
Wayne, John, 83
wealth, 22, 117. *See also*
    inequality; poverty
welfare reform, 52, 69. *See also*
    inequality; poverty
"What America Would Be Like
    Without Blacks" (Ellison),
    43
*What Manner of Man: A
    Biography of Martin Luther
    King, Jr.* (Bennet), 37
Where We Stand: Class Matters
    (hooks), 27
White, Ronnie, 69
White Citizens Council, 99
White Knights of Columbus, 50
whiteness, 47–48, 50, 51, 125n.4.
    See also blacks; skin color